CHASING TRAVER'S MAGIC

A Journey into the World of Fly Fishing for Trout

John Highlen

Artwork by Julie Highlen

NATURAL CONNECTIONS
Deerton, Michigan

Published by Natural Connections 2024

ISBN 979-8-9900307-0-1 (soft cover)

Printed in the United States of America

Also by John Highlen

Touching the Wild U.P.

Porkies Wilderness Wanderings

To my many mentors, in trout fishing and in life.

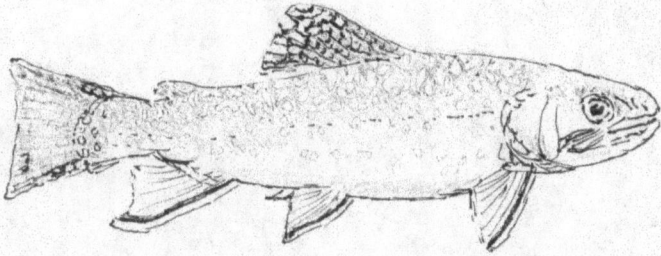

The universe is full of magical things patiently
waiting for our wits to grow sharper.

—Eden Phillpotts

The universe is full of magical things patiently
waiting for our wits to grow sharper.

—Eden Phillpotts

CONTENTS

ACKNOWLEDGEMENTS

I am indebted to my wife, Julie, for once again lending her artistic talents to my writing project. Having an in-house artist/illustrator is a blessing, but I'm sure I'm running up a sizeable tab in those regards.

A special Thank You to our friend, Barb Osbon, for graciously agreeing to be the proofreading wizard on this writing project. I appreciate her patience and attention to detail. Especially those punctuation details that I tend to screw up so often.

Many thanks to my friend, Jim Jenkin, for turning me on to some great flies, and some great places to fish with them. I also want to thank the many others that have worked and fished with me through this fly fishing journey.

Most importantly, I thank God for placing me in a country where I am free to pursue my dreams, and for moving me to an area where the magic of those dreams can be a daily adventure.

INTRODUCTION

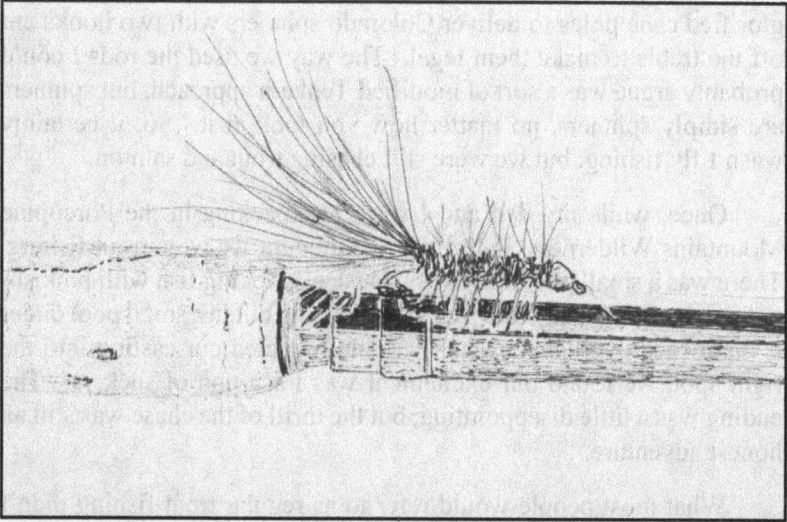

I love trout. I began chasing Traver's magic long before I even knew John Voelker—aka Robert Traver—or his book *Trout Magic* even existed. As a kid, I dreamed of trout fishing. In some ways, you could probably say that I fantasized about it. Though I had never actually seen many outside of a magazine or aquarium, sleek, wild trout swam through my mind as vividly as Saturday morning cartoons. Any stream was potential trout water, even though in southern Michigan where I grew up, real trout water was some three hours away. Rumors of more local trout floated around at times, but real trout water wasn't a local thing. In my young mind, though, moving water held trout. It was that simple.

When I was in my early teens, I bought a four-piece pack rod and ultra-light Daiwa reel specifically for back-country trout expeditions.

I don't recall ever actually using that outfit for trout, but it fueled many a trout dream just the same.

My dad and I chased salmon and steelhead on the Platte River, near Honor, Michigan, with fly rods, which we simply used as glorified cane poles to deliver Colorado spinners with two hooks cut off the treble to make them legal. The way we used the rods I could probably argue was a sort of modified Tenkara approach, but spinners are simply spinners, no matter how you look at it. So, it certainly wasn't fly fishing, but we were still chasing trout and salmon.

Once, while my dad and I were backpacking in the Porcupine Mountains Wilderness State Park, we thought we were trout fishing. There was a small pod of six or seven sleek-looking fish with pinkish-red stripes along their sides that were hanging out in a small pool under a slight rock overhang. When we finally dialed our casting into the right spot, we found our excitement was for a pod of suckers. The ending was a little disappointing, but the thrill of the chase was still an honest adventure.

What most people would refer to as regular trout fishing didn't really become a reality until I went away to college. Going to Michigan Tech, in the western Upper Peninsula (UP), I had the Keweenaw as my outdoor playground for four years. I didn't have much time available to fish, but my friend Tim and I did slip off to a small stream now and then to drench a few crawlers or run a Mepps spinner through some deeper holes. We never caught anything sizeable, but it was trout fishing nonetheless, and it kept my dream pump primed for future trout-induced wanderings.

My wife, Julie, and I did a few similar forays with similar results as my trout quest continued early in our life together. Then, trout fishing took a backseat to countless other endeavors as we were raising our family and learning small-scale farming, but the fascination with trout and trout water never faded. I still often dreamed of trout fishing and eagerly read about it whenever I could. Then, when our youngest daughter was away at college in the Upper Peninsula, I took up fly fishing—for trout of course. My fly fishing trout quest wasn't a full-fledged passion at first. It was more of an interest, or maybe it would be more appropriate to say it was an occasional indulgence. I didn't get to do it often, because good trout water was still three or more hours north of our farm, but I would squeeze in a short fishing stop on my way home from college visits or work weekends at our Upper Peninsula cabin whenever I could. I hesitate to actually call what I was doing *trout fishing*. It was more realistically fly casting, or attempted fly casting, to be completely honest. I didn't catch much on those first short fishing ventures, but I was a trout fisherman just the same. A fly fisherman, in fact, learning fly casting and humility at the same time. I did manage to catch a few, though. A few small trout and several trees of various sizes. I was finally living, even if it was infrequently, the dreams of my youth. Or at least I was beginning to. I still wasn't catching the fish of my dreams, but I was honestly fly fishing for trout, and it was satisfying an inner craving that I had been carrying around for years. Not that it really mattered, but I was convinced that size and numbers would come in time if I simply kept pursuing the dream.

I have heard it said that the only way to ensure that you don't get your line tangled or snag your fly on a branch is to not fly fish. Well, I have chosen to fish. So, I inevitably get tangled or decorate a branch now and then. Actually, the truth is that it happens more often than I care to admit. Sometimes it happens when I'm in the middle of what is going to be a perfect cast. With a very light tippet, the instantaneous tug while I'm coming forward from my back cast is so minute that it doesn't even disrupt the cast. As I'm congratulating myself on such a delicate presentation, I realize it was delicate because the only thing I presented was the end of my tippet. Other times, when I'm trying to free a snag and the fly finally pops loose, the ensuing tangle is such a god-awful mess that it consumes my entire tippet and a good portion of the leader. There's even been a time or two that the trainwreck included my fly line, rod, and one of the eyelets. I haven't quite come to grips with the fact that those things are more or less a normal part of fly fishing, but I have gotten quieter, and a little more subtle, with my response.

The pursuit of my trout and fly fishing dream eventually blossomed into a move north to the Upper Peninsula after my engineering job of twenty-five years evaporated one day and I found my options wide open. Moving to the Upper Peninsula wasn't driven solely by trout fishing, but it was certainly one of the factors. We started looking for a home in the Keweenaw, my old college haunt,

15

then spread out the search when that didn't seem to be panning out. We eventually found a place in the central UP, right in Robert Traver country. Even beyond Lake Superior, water defines this area. Rivers, creeks, and streams abound. Most of them hold at least some trout, even if they're not known as being trout water. There are so many trout fishing options now that it's hard to decide where to start or where to focus. Regardless, most of these waters are fertile, dark north woods waters, full of mystery and invitation. As far as I'm concerned, there probably isn't a truly bad option. Even the poorest of trout streams are still tantalizing places to explore and dream. The focus of my pursuit is not just trout but the magic, as Traver referred to it. Trout magic.

I can't honestly say that I know exactly what defines trout magic or how you know when you've caught it, but I'm pretty sure that I've caught at least a few glimpses of it. Just like the trout themselves, the magic is fluidly elusive and often difficult to detect. Regardless, I've certainly been enjoying the chase.

OPENING DAY

I missed the opening day of the first trout season after we moved to real trout country. It was a bright sunny day. Water was running high, fast, and cold. It was also our first spring at our new home, so we were working on a major to-do list. Those were my excuses. I didn't feel too bad, though. Mostly because I had never participated in a trout season opening day in my life. So, I really had no idea what I was missing. Now that I was living in brook trout country, I was hoping to get out on the water somewhere on opening day, but I had heard that opening day in the Upper Peninsula typically isn't all that great because it's too early up here. Streams are too high, fast, and cold. As a result, fish tend to be sluggish and hard to find. But regardless of the reasons and excuses, and despite the fact that I had been looking forward to the trout opener for several months, the day slipped by, and I did nothing about it. That evening, I was lamenting my lack of action and wishing I had that day back for a do-over. It was only one day, but it felt like I had missed a milestone.

The following year, I was determined not to miss out on opening day, whether the fishing was good or not. After some internal debate, I decided to try Buck Bay Creek, just upstream of Au Train Lake. When I arrived, I found the snow in that area was considerably deeper than it was at home. I had to park my truck in a snowbank along the road and slog my way into the small river mouth campground and songbird nature trail that follows the stream. The songbird trail was packed down but narrow, so stepping off into snow up to knee-deep was a regular occurrence while I worked my way upstream to get beyond the slow-flow area of the mouth. Once I traded the trail for the riverbank, I found a few trouty-looking holes, but being in a relatively open area, they were in direct bright sunlight, so I wasn't able to entice any fish into action. On a dreary day, it may have been a different story. But it wasn't a dreary day.

Upstream, as the streamside forest thickened, shaded water became more prevalent, but there was also a considerable amount of brush, branches, and wood, both in and out of the creek. Snow was also more consistently knee-deep, except for the areas where it extended up as high as my waist. It was early enough in the day that the crusted snow was still firm enough from nighttime temperatures to support about half of my weight. Sometimes I could stay on top of the snow for a step or two before one leg would plunge in at least thigh-deep. Other times I would only make it half of a step before the plunge. I had been planning on fishing, not working out, but at least the scenery was better than at a gym. And it smelled better.

The creek itself had a mostly sandy bottom, with pockets of clean spawning gravel. It was decorated with a healthy amount of wood in various forms. Water depth and speed were readily fishable. Throughout my couple of hours of fishing explorations, I found an abundance of trout water but no trout. Not even a brief sighting. Still, it was better than working in the yard or sitting at my desk, wondering what I was missing. If I had stayed home, I would have missed the magic of a bright spring day on the water.

On the slog back to my truck, I passed a scattering of grouse feathers, marking the event of someone's meal. Melted snow obscured the details of the diner's tracks, but I couldn't help but wonder if it was the tale of another creature that was unable to find a trout.

As opening day rolled around again, even though fishing a small creek had not previously resulted in a fish in my net, I still liked the idea of smaller water during that time of high, fast water. I reasoned that smaller streams would likely tend to warm up a little sooner than bigger streams, too. With that mindset, I hiked into Silver Creek, near the east side of the Rock River Canyon Wilderness. As I stepped into the wilderness area, I was welcomed by the drumming of a grouse filtering through the forest. The tension of everyday life slipped away as I thought about how the natural world was still doing what the natural world was designed to do, whether we are there to witness it or not. I was there to not only witness it but to participate in the ongoing drama.

Before reaching Silver Creek, I crossed a small un-named creek running clear and clean. The sandy bottom was nearly white, giving the creek an exotic air. I briefly thought about following its flow, just to explore, but decided to stick with my original plan, and followed an even smaller creek that was flowing down what used to be a two-track, heading over a rise toward my original destination. I couldn't help laughing at myself for eyeing the foot-wide cascading flow for fish. My boyhood mentality that flowing water is trout water is often hard for me to shake. Sometimes I think that certain aspects of a boyhood mentality are probably an asset. So, I don't try very hard to shake my fondness for moving water. Trouty or not.

My first glimpse of the lower stretch of Silver Creek caught me by surprise. In my vocabulary, I would call it a river. In fact, it was similar in size to the Rock River which was just down around the next bend. The other thing that caught my attention was how much clearer it was than other area streams of that size. Based on that, I assumed it was primarily spring-fed, and the spring or springs didn't bubble up in a swamp somewhere. I explored my way down to its confluence with the Rock, took off my daypack, and began assembling my fly rod.

When I tried attaching my reel, things didn't seem to be fitting up for some reason. A quick inspection showed that the reason was a bent-up foot on the reel. I had no idea how it had gotten bent, but it didn't really matter at that point. It just needed to be fixed. I pulled my Leatherman knock-off out of my pack and went to work unbending or re-bending things the best I could without breaking anything. The finished product wasn't pretty, but it worked.

As I worked my way upstream, I began noticing the lack of readily fishable holding water. That was especially true up in what I would call a canyon. I estimated the steep banks to be sixty to eighty feet tall. There were plenty of big hemlocks and plenty of big hemlock blowdowns. Many were in the stream. Great fish habitat. Not great fishing habitat. Between blowdowns and small waterfalls, wading the creek wasn't working out so well. Climbing the steep banks to avoid obstacles wasn't working out so well either. After a few hours of vigorous exercise, I conceded that the fish were going to stay where they were and climbed the steep bank one more time to access easier bushwacking along the rim.

On the way back to my truck, I had the only trout sighting of the day. As I followed the little trickle running down the old logging trail, I surprised a six-inch brook trout. Actually, we surprised each other. I briefly toyed with the idea of letting it calm down and seeing if I could get it to take a fly, but I decided that it was already stressed enough. It didn't need me adding to its predicament. I couldn't decide if calling a fish sighting a success would be considered a step up or a step down in my fly fishing career. I thought about it a bit on my way to the truck and finally concluded that if I kept it to myself, I could call it whatever I wanted. I called the day a success.

I entered the next new year with high hopes and optimism. By mid-March, with the COVID-19 buzz getting louder by the minute, my optimism and enthusiasm were waning. Still, I figured that we would just need to hang on for a month or two and that mess would be behind us. Early in April, in order to help boost my outlook on things, I went out and purchased my new fishing license. My thought was that at least the prospect of going fishing would give me something to look forward to. By the late April opening day of trout season, gloom and doom panic was still in full swing. People were hoarding toilet paper for some unknown reason. The price of everything was escalating and economic news was where the toilet paper should have been. I made a rash decision and opted out of opening day fishing. For one thing, I didn't feel right about spending money on gas to drive somewhere to fish. For another thing, the whole situation was just dragging me down into a horrendously pissy mood and I simply didn't feel like going. I found myself wondering if I had made a big mistake in even buying a fishing license in the first place. The way things were looking, I might not get to use it at all. As the sun disappeared that evening, however, I was lamenting the loss of the opportunity that I had just foolishly slammed the door on.

After a few more Sundays of Pastor Kelto reminding me that there was a much higher power than COVID in control of the world – the universe, in fact – I finally started pulling loose from the news media stranglehold. Much worse things than the current virus had happened in the past and the sun was still coming up every morning because the earth was still spinning in its appointed rotation, right where it needed to be to support the plethora of life in and around us. There was more to fishing season than opening day and more to life than the apparent gloom of the present.

Another trip around the sun brought me back to the idea of looking for trout in Silver Creek again. On the way in, I made a short pass by the Rock River to check on a couple of holes where I had found good fishing in the past. Sometime during the previous season, sand had migrated into the area – lots of sand – and filled in most of the old holes, completely changing the river. From a fishing standpoint, the sand had completely screwed everything up. I wanted to see if the river had begun cleaning itself up yet.

It had not. At least as far as I could tell, nothing had really improved. Out of habit, and maybe just because of the connection I had developed with the river, I went ahead and fished the only hole that was still a hole. It was one of my favorite holes anyway. I assumed that there were at least a few fish hiding somewhere in its murky depths, but they stayed there, so I was never able to confirm my assumption. Shortly before I conceded my loss of the first round of opening day, I heard a ruckus in the brush behind me. Two guys were bushwacking their way toward me, obviously intent on fishing the hole I was standing in the edge of. They abruptly stopped and had a quiet conversation, apparently having finally noticed me standing there. Without saying anything, or even acknowledging my presence, they retreated. Based on the net and spinning gear that I glimpsed, I assumed they were planning to work over the hole in pursuit of steelhead. Once the noise of their bushwacking disappeared, I quietly moved on toward my original destination.

Light rain was turning to snow, so I suppressed my urge to play in the smaller creeks that I passed. Silver Creek was running faster than I had hoped, but it wasn't bad, considering the time of year. The bends and logjams that I was sure held trout were woody debris fortresses. I made several attempts at fishing their fringes, but the early-season fish were staying put in their hideouts. A couple of small fish of just a few inches in length did momentarily dart out from cover, but I wasn't interested in catching them any more than they were interested in being caught.

During my logjam explorations, I did spot a rainbow – likely a steelhead – that I estimated to be eighteen inches long, but it too was hidden away. From the south bank, I could clearly see it through a small wood-framed window holding tight under a large log. From out in the water, its hideout was guarded by a cage wall of vertical sticks. Multiple presentations of multiple flies produced nothing but the rhythmic waving of its tail. It just held there in its sanctuary, probably waiting for me to leave. I finally obliged and continued upstream until the blowdowns became too much of a barrier. The snow had reverted back to light rain somewhere in the course of my stream wanderings. I wasn't sure if the lack of success was due to the day or the fish or me, but it didn't necessarily matter anyway. With a slight drip falling from the bill of my hat, I conceded yet another opening day and headed toward my truck.

I had been looking forward to that day since sometime back in the cold and snow of prime winter, but as I left the stream, it didn't really feel like opening day of trout season. It felt like just a day that I chose to go play in the water. April weather had been mild, leaving little trace of winter in the woods, so cabin fever feelings had already melted away with the winter white. Maybe that's why the day hadn't felt as special as opening day normally did. Regardless, I had ventured out and enjoyed a little catch-and-release fishing. The catching part was just lacking.

Spring is often challenging here in the Upper Peninsula. The last few weeks before the regular trout season begins, I tend to feel restless.

Snowshoeing and skiing are done, but there is still too much slushy – sometimes crusty – snow for hiking or cross-country exploring. It's not yet paddling season and trout season is still in the distance. Realistically, I'm typically confined to walking the paved road from our house to the "town" of Deerton and back for exercise, because our dirt sideroad is too wet and muddy for an enjoyable walk. Continually repeating the three-mile round-trip walk makes me feel like a dog pacing in a long kennel. I can see the real outside world and can even smell it. I just can't quite reach it yet. In the restlessness, some days I'm annoyed or agitated. Other days I'm simply resigned to indifferent acceptance. Every year I tell myself that I need to get into steelhead fishing during this transition season. Some years, maple syrup season helps bridge the gap and the wait doesn't seem so long. Regardless, it always feels like I'm anxiously waiting.

Last year for opening day, I gave the Laughing Whitefish a try, up near the falls. As always, I enjoyed playing in the water and getting a participant's view from the base of the falls. Through the course of my fishing, I caught water, a few rocks, and several sticks, though I didn't hook any trees. Plenty of action, just not with fish. A typical opening day, here in the Upper Peninsula.

For opening day this year, I had plans to look for a sizable brown trout in one of the near-home rivers, but when I arrived, it was obvious that several other people had the same idea. There was probably room for me to slip in somewhere where I was neither bothering nor being bothered by others, but I opted to go someplace quieter. With conditions not being what I would call optimal, I didn't want to go far out of my way just to wet a fly. So, even though it hadn't quite recovered from an influx of sand that occurred a few years ago, I stopped by my home water. The new normal still wasn't good, but it was convenient, and I was there, so I put on my new waders and rigged up my rod.

The first bend hole had somewhat reformed, and I could see a decent-size fish hugging the bottom at the back of the hole. Unfortunately, there was a submerged log across the river just upstream of the fish, blocking a fly from reaching the mark. After a few hopeful casts, I decided to leave that fish to lethargically hide behind its log, and I moved upstream to a place where I have often found success.

At my planned success spot, there was a bushy, semi-broken alder branch obstructing success. It was touching the water right in the middle of the prime fishing zone. If I cast behind the branch, by the time my fly sank to where it needed to be, it was out of the hole. If I cast to the front of the hole, by the time my fly was down to the bottom, my line was in the branch. If I added any more weight, it would just act like an anchor. As I pondered the situation, I came up with two possible solutions. Wade in far enough to break off the offending branch, then give the hole some time to rest before fishing, or go back to the first hole where I at least knew there was a fish. I don't like altering river structure to suit my personal desires, so I headed back downstream.

The fish, which looked to be at least a foot long, was still holding behind its log. Over the course of the next hour, I labored to get a fly to that fish. At one point, I even found myself consciously trying to *will* the fly to the fish. It didn't work and the fish apparently didn't care. There were at least a few casts where I was sure my fly went right past the trout's nose without inducing the slightest reaction. I wasn't sure if it didn't like what I was offering or if it was simply being antagonistic.

At that point, the water temperature that was keeping the fish lethargic was also giving me a slight chill. The extra jacket that I had declared unnecessary when I left the car was beginning to sound like a good idea. With the next thought, I decided to go home to a warm house and have chicken for dinner while another opening day settled into darkness. Fish would be for another day, but probably not an opening day.

WADING WET

A t the beginning of an outdoors adventure, you never know exactly what to expect. But I guess that's part of what makes it an adventure. My wife, Julie, and I had decided to spend a summer day fishing for trout on the Platte River in northern Michigan. Out of habit, I drove us to a familiar stretch of river near a small rustic campground on M-72. I had fished it many times in the past with my dad and some of his friends, but that was in the Fall for coho salmon or early Spring for steelhead. Summer fishing there for local trout would be a new twist for me. This was prior to my more recent fly fishing endeavors, so worms and Mepps spinners were the tackle of choice.

We only had one pair of waders. Julie's feet tend to get cold easily, so she was the natural choice to wear the waders. Besides, it seemed too warm for waders to me, so I did the gentlemanly thing and offered them to Julie. I donned an old pair of running shoes and waded wet.

That part wasn't new. I had plenty of experience wading wet. Once, on a Thanksgiving weekend backpacking trip to Pennsylvania, I was more or less forced to wade wet. It was just cold enough for a little bit of snow to be lingering on the ground. More than a dusting but not quite enough to actually be measurable. Overall, the woods looked white, but there were still dried leaves visible. The trail crossed a stream about twenty feet wide, but there was no bridge—obviously a summer trail. The air temperature was probably just below freezing. Not too cold but cold enough that I didn't want wet hiking boots the rest of the day. So, I did the only sensible thing to do. I took off my boots and socks, rolled up my pants, and offered to carry Julie across —you do that sort of thing when you're relatively newly married. By the way, it's not easy carrying someone across a cold, gravel-bottom stream when you're barefooted. Anyway, Julie took a picture of me making a second crossing with our backpacks. I still have the framed picture in my office as evidence of my chivalry and occasional lack of sense.

Another time, I was bird hunting with a friend named Dave at his family cabin on the Escanaba River. We got an early dusting of snow one day while we were making a big loop, looking for grouse. We had gone downstream quite a distance, crossed over the river at a dam, and were working our way up the other side toward a bridge that was probably at least a half mile past the cabin. It was a slow day for birds. Not that the birds were slow. The couple that we actually saw shot out through the thick brush like they came out of a catapult. We just weren't finding many grouse. So, when we got to the point where we could see the cabin across the river, it looked warmly inviting. We still had quite a hike through thick woods up to the bridge, and the dam we had crossed was about as far in the other direction.

That was when Dave said, "Let's just wade across to the cabin and call it good." The river didn't look like it was more than knee deep, but the fast-moving, icy water covered a bed of rocks ranging in size from marbles to bowling balls. Without answering, I sized up the situation. I estimated the width of the river to be at least sixty feet. As I was wondering how we would manage to dry out soaking wet leather boots, Dave brushed the snow off a large rock, sat down, and began untying his bootlaces. That was the easy answer. Don't get the boots wet in the first place. It seemed like a reasonable plan. Take off our boots and socks, roll up our pants and long underwear, wade across sixty feet or so of icy, fast-moving water on varying-size slippery rocks, and emerge barefooted on the far snow-covered bank. Being a guy in my early twenties, it made perfect sense to me (Julie would probably tell you that more than thirty years haven't changed things much in that respect).

As we started across, Dave turned to me and said, "The trick is to keep your eyes on the far bank. If you look down at the water, you'll be in trouble." I didn't ask what exactly he meant by "trouble", but I figured it had something to do with getting our boots wet even though they were hanging around our necks by their laces.

I made it to about the middle of the river without incident. I could feel the current pushing against my legs, but my balance seemed fine. I didn't really notice the rocks. Probably because my feet were quickly going numb. I felt confident. Maybe even a little brashly mountain mannish. Then I confidently looked down.

Water rushed by in a blur. My feet and legs stung. My head began to spin like I had indulged in a few too many beers. As the door of confidence was slamming shut, panic rushed in. As I was about to go down, I looked up to see where Dave was and caught sight of the far riverbank. The instant my eyes locked onto the cabin and trees along the river, clarity calmly took hold. The cold, the dizziness, the panic, gone. I was once again in a crisp Upper Peninsula afternoon. Relieved, I kept my eyes glued on the cabin side of the river as I waded the rest of the way there. I decided not to mention the incident to Dave but tucked that lesson away. I was sure that one would prove useful somewhere down the line.

So, for me and Julie, that day on the Platte was pleasant, but the fishing wasn't much to talk about. It didn't take long for Julie to start losing interest. She wanted to move on upstream, but I wasn't quite done with our present fishing spot. It was a straight stretch of stream where I could see for quite a distance, so I told her to go ahead and leapfrog past me and try upstream. She got out of the water and disappeared down the well-worn streamside trail. The brush was thick, so she was out of sight within a few steps. Every couple of casts I would look upstream. No Julie. After several upstream glances, I decided she must have had a nature call. With waders on, that's no simple call to answer, so I kept working on the deep run that stretched out in front of me.

When I had done a thorough enough job exploring that stretch of water, I decided I had better go check on Julie. It had probably been about twenty minutes since she had disappeared down the trail. I didn't have to go far to find her. As soon as I saw her, I remembered that I should have warned her that some of the black patches that looked a little muddy were actually pretty nasty muck holes. The kind where boots can disappear forever. Anyway, there she was, about knee-deep in black, smelly muck. Her blushed complexion, erratic breathing, and sweat-soaked strands of hair sticking to her forehead told me she had been struggling there for a bit. The look on her face told me that any comments that came to mind would be better off kept there. I managed to hold my comments, but I lost control of my senses and committed one of the cardinal sins of male/female relationships. I snickered. The only thing that saved me was that she still needed my help to get out. I was pardoned. At least temporarily. I also had the truck keys, so I had that going for me, too.

The muck hole was big enough in diameter that I couldn't get enough leverage from the edge, so I ended up scrounging up a couple of sturdy logs that were light enough to carry and laid them along each side of Julie. I walked out to her with one foot on each log, grabbed her around the waist, and pulled straight up. Fortunately, the muck gave out before my back did. Her feet were no longer in the boot part of the waders, but at least the waders were still on, she was free from the muck, and there was no immediate retaliation. It appeared that I would eventually even be forgiven. I did get a little bit of muck on me, but it washed right off as soon as I stepped back into the river.

There have also been times when wading wet didn't mean that I wasn't wearing waders. Once, when I was in college at Michigan Tech, my friend Tim and I were doing some Spring fishing on a small stream in the Keweenaw. The water was high and looking a little like milky tea as Upper Peninsula streams often do that time of year. So, we were really more exploring than fishing, but the other option was homework, so we went "fishing". At one point, we decided that we really needed to be on the other side of the stream, so we searched for a suitable location to cross. With the water clarity being what it was, it was impossible to determine the depth, so we just started trying different spots, mostly at random. In one of my attempts, I got to the middle of the flow and the bottom flattened out. It felt pretty level and solid. The water level was still several inches from the top of my waders, so I figured that I had it made. As I glanced back to tell Tim we were good to go, I took a confident step forward right into a hole. Fortunately, I was wearing a belt on my waders, which was something I didn't always do in those days, so the breath-stealing water didn't gush down my waders. It was metered in slowly as I frantically flailed the air with my arms and tried to backpedal. Only about a quart of water made it into each boot. At that point, we gave up trying to cross. The other side didn't seem so inviting any longer.

When I was a kid, I started exploring rivers with hand-me-down waders from my dad. They were a little big for me, which made the belt even more important, and they had already seen their better days. At one point, the hot glue stick patches became too numerous to readily count, so it was difficult to tell if one (or more) was missing. I could certainly tell as soon as I stepped in the water, though. Especially on those very early- and late-season ventures. Stopping every hour or so to empty my waders was a common practice. At times I wasn't even sure why I wore them at all, although I suppose they did do a pretty good job of keeping the mud and muck off my pants and socks.

A few years ago, I had an opportunity to get involved in an electro-shocking outing with some graduate students and a biology professor from NMU, along with a couple of forest service fisheries folks. We were catching trout and salmon in order to collect some data. My job was to push and guide the "barge" that held the generator and various other equipment upstream. Sometimes when shocked fish were a little too numerous for the two netters to handle, I would leave the barge in the hands of the person guiding the bow and grab a net to help capture fish.

On one of those occasions, a large rainbow trout was getting away downstream, with me in hot pursuit. I was so focused on the fish that I didn't notice the hole I was stepping into as I netted the trout. Even though I had a belt around my waders, a considerable amount of November river water flowed over the top and worked its way down, soaking me from chest to toes. I got out of the river, emptied a gallon or so of water out of each boot, and put the waders back on.

Not long after that incident, another large rainbow that wasn't quite stunned enough to be netted started to make a downstream getaway. Without even thinking about it, the shocker spun around, put the electrode in the water a couple of feet from my leg, and pulled the trigger. With my waders wet inside and out, and a slight leak at the knees completing the circuit, it felt like I had just put both knees against a high-voltage electric fence. If I hadn't been leaning on the barge at the time, I would have gone for a swim. I can't say that it was truly painful, but the experience was definitely extremely unenjoyable. It's something that I certainly do not want to repeat.

It seems like I've always had a natural attraction to water. Or maybe water has always had a natural attraction to me. I find myself getting wet on a pretty regular basis. Boots don't seem to help much either. When I wear ten-inch-tall boots, I find eleven-inch deep water. So, I splurged on a pair of sixteen-inch L.L. Bean hunting boots. They're great boots. The only problem is that now I seem to have a knack for finding seventeen-inch-deep streams and puddles. And as I've already mentioned, waders don't always make a difference either—I'm still trying to fix the leaks in the knees instead of springing for a new pair.

I guess it doesn't really matter. Whether I get wet or not, it's the experience that's important. That day on the Platte River, Julie and I both got wet (and a bit mucky). The fishing was fun, even though we didn't catch many trout and the few we did catch were small. The important thing was that we spent an adventurous day outside playing in a beautiful stretch of river that I hadn't visited in several years. I spent the day recalling and reliving a lot of fond memories of fishing there with my dad when I was a kid. Maybe more importantly, as with most fishing excursions, my collection of fond memories increased that day, too. They were just a little damp.

FIRST TROUT ON A FLY

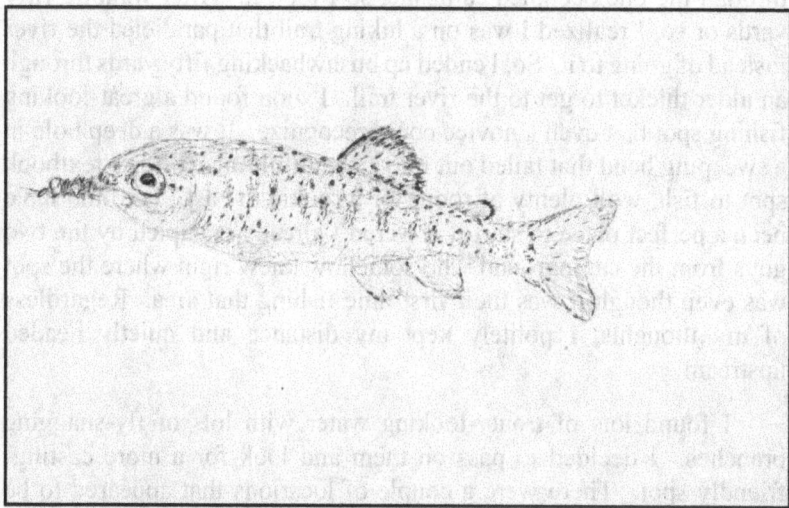

My first fly fishing venture wasn't a big success by normal standards, but I've never been known for normal standards. I was fishing a stretch of the Pigeon River in the heart of northern Michigan elk country. Part of the reason I picked the Pigeon as a starting point was the possibility of catching a glimpse of one of the big cervids as I was stalking along the river. The other reason was that it was only a short jaunt off the highway as I headed home from a work weekend at our family cabin in the Upper Peninsula.

As I was cumbersomely rigging up my rod in the small county park campground where I had parked, a couple of younger guys zipped in with an old pick-up truck, parked off to the side by the outhouses, threw their stuff together, and headed toward the river. I tried to politely ask them a couple of basic questions about fishing that stretch, but one of them blurted out that it was their first time there, as they shot past me and made a beeline toward somewhere they somehow knew they needed to be.

There was only one obvious trail (it had a sign) that didn't go through the one occupied campsite, so I took it. After walking fifty yards or so, I realized I was on a hiking trail that paralleled the river instead of going to it. So, I ended up bushwhacking fifty yards through an alder thicket to get to the river trail. I soon found a great-looking fishing spot that even a novice could recognize. It was a deep hole in a sweeping bend that tailed out into a beautiful run. It was a textbook spot to fish, with plenty of room for a rookie to cast. It would have been a perfect place to start if it weren't already occupied by the two guys from the campground who somehow knew right where the spot was even though it was their first time fishing that area. Regardless of my thoughts, I politely kept my distance and quietly headed upstream.

I found lots of trouty-looking water with lots of fly-snagging branches. I decided to pass on them and look for a more casting-friendly spot. There were a couple of locations that appeared to be more forgiving, so I splashed a black Wooly Bugger around to no avail. The fly fishing videos had looked a lot easier than what I was experiencing. While walking the trail to the next likely-looking access spot, I learned why not to carry your rod trailing behind you, especially when you're using a 6x tippet. There was a light, quick tug on the rod as I passed a large spruce tree. I looked back to see my rod dragging the line, leader, and tippet, minus the Wooly Bugger. A quick frisking of the spruce turned up nothing. I felt slighted. Losing a fly to a fish or to a snag while executing a highly technical casting maneuver, that would be fine. That would make for a fun story to tell my family and friends. But losing my fly in a spruce tree while I wasn't even actually fishing, that was just depressing.

Daylight was fading to that pre-dusk dull you often get on an overcast day. I decided not to bother tying on another fly and began just following the river back toward my truck, quietly observing whatever the river was willing to show me. With my focus intent on the water, I didn't notice the small herd of elk grazing in a small meadow just beyond the far riverbank. I assumed they were peacefully grazing in the meadow, although I didn't actually witness it. What I witnessed was tawny-colored bodies with dark necks thundering off into the forest, popping branches as they disappeared. At first, it was another disappointment, but I reminded myself that I had at least seen some elk, even if it was just at the last second.

I set my sights on next time, picked a trail heading in the direction of the campground, and followed it. The trail came out right next to the one occupied campsite, where three people were sitting around a blazing campfire. As they looked up from the fire, one of them asked if I had caught anything. When I admitted that I hadn't, they responded with, "Really? Nothing?!" in what sounded like a genuinely surprised tone, which I perceived to mean something to the effect of *nobody ever gets skunked here*. That made me feel better.

So, I had to go back. If nothing else, to at least redeem myself in my own mind. It was late afternoon when I arrived at an empty campground. I felt better not having a peanut gallery to contend with. That meant the river was likely mine, too. I headed straight to one of the relatively easy casting locations that I remembered from the previous visit. It was a small, dark run in the shade of a large spruce. I tied on a small bead-head nymph with a yellow indicator about eighteen inches above the fly. As I was putting away my fly box and stashing my nippers in my upper pocket, I dropped the nymph into the shallow water at my feet and watched it begin tumbling downstream across the colored gravel. Just as I finished zipping my fishing vest pocket, I felt a slight pulse in my line and it began dancing around. I raised my rod tip high enough to bring the nymph clear of the water and there it was, a two-inch-long brown trout, cleanly hooked through the upper lip. I quickly looked around to make sure nobody was watching, and then I laughed. It was my first official trout caught on a fly. Not that I didn't appreciate the little fish, but I had always expected it to be a more momentous occasion. Well, at least if anyone asked, I could just tell them the truth and say that I caught a small brown. I just wouldn't elaborate.

Somehow, knowing that I wasn't going to get skunked for the day seemed to take the edge off my doubts. I had evidence that trout did actually exist in that stretch of river and that I could actually catch one—kind of. I had a renewed sense of anticipation as I unhooked the fry and dropped the nymph at the head of the run with a somewhat clumsy cast. Then I attentively followed the yellow indicator as it bobbed along. I felt a sense that something was imminent. A second cast. Anticipation heightened. I became absorbed in the moment and the rhythm of the routine. Somewhere in the next several casts, it happened. The indicator disappeared into the dark current. Even though that was what I was anticipating, what I was hoping would happen, it still caught me by surprise. Fortunately, the trout took care of setting the hook because I never thought to. I just stood there for the first few seconds watching the line dance around and feeling the pulses coming through the rod. Then I somewhat frantically pulled the fish in, fearing that it would get off. A five-inch rainbow came to hand. Not a big fish. In fact, not even a legal keeper. But it was a lively, honest-to-goodness wild trout caught on a fly that I had purposefully cast to a specific spot in the river. It was a small success but a success all the same. My confidence swelled as I began thinking about the next fish. So, I made my way downstream to the open bend hole that I remembered from my previous visit, carefully carrying my rod in front of me so that I could see to keep it clear of the branches.

At first, I stood a ways off to study the situation and lay out a plan because, based on my reading, that's what people who fly fish do. Nothing was rising, so I dismissed the dry fly option. The nymph that I already had tied on had already worked once, twice actually, so what better place to start? To get to what I believed to be a good casting location downstream of the hole, I crossed the river well above the hole so as not to spook any likely candidates, then carefully picked my way through the tangle of alders guarding the river. Once in position, I pondered things for a few more minutes, mostly because I was afraid to make a crappy first cast and blow the whole deal. After taking a somewhat educated guess on how far above the nymph to locate my indicator, I made a few false casts and dropped the fly more or less where I wanted it. I was pleasantly surprised and a bit relieved. This might actually work out. Before I could pat myself on the back, the indicator was through the hole and floating swiftly past me. I sent it back to the head of the hole again. And again. Not sure what else to do, I repeated the process for about twenty minutes with the same result. I began wondering if maybe I underestimated the depth and wasn't getting the fly down to the bottom. Maybe a different fly. Maybe I wasn't in quite the right position for a clean drift. Maybe I had already spooked all the hole's occupants and was just practicing my casting. Regardless, the splattering of small clouds assembled above me was showing orange and red from the sun that was apparently setting somewhere behind the trees. That's when I noticed the slight breeze bringing in the evening chill. I was sure that hole held trout, but it looked like it was going to keep them to itself.

I pulled my camera out of my large vest pocket, snapped a couple of glowing cloud shots, and decided I'd better get the remaining three-hour drive home underway. Waders aren't exactly stealthy, but I did my best to sneak quietly back to my truck, hoping for another elk encounter. Not only were there no elk encounters, there were no people encounters either. The campground was still empty. I had a success story to tell and nobody to tell it to. Well, that's not quite true. I'd be telling my wife when I got home. She has the job of listening to all my stories. Sometimes she listens half-heartedly, but she listens. It's part of the "for better or worse" clause.

As darkness followed the wisps of cooling air, I clipped off the veteran nymph, hooked it on the drying patch on my vest, and broke down my rod. In hindsight, I should have fished the nymph a little deeper before I left, or maybe tried swinging a streamer. Next time. Next time is always the one where things are really going to come together. The stars will align, prayers will be answered, previous lessons will really start to settle in and make sense. Next time. This time was good, but it's always nice to have a next time on the horizon to provide fuel for dreams and energy for getting through the day-to-day details. Even after a good day on the water, for some reason, next time often seems to be the best time.

HOME WATER

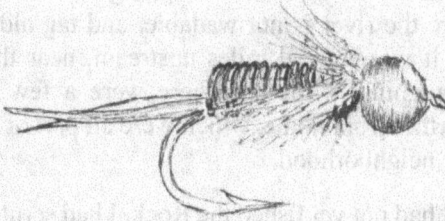

E ven though the Laughing Whitefish River runs along a portion
of our north property line, this area really is not trout water. It's
typically too warm. I'm told that steelhead do pass through on
their way to more habitable water, but timing can be tricky. The more
common inhabitants are suckers and creek chubs. Bass are more likely
than trout. These days, beavers and otters are more likely than trout,
too. In order for me to reach trout water on the Laughing Whitefish,
it requires about a forty-minute round-about drive. About halfway
through that scenic drive, I encounter the Rock River. That is what I
consider to be my Home Water. Here in Michigan's Upper Peninsula,
most people consider anything within about an hour's drive to be local,
which for me includes a number of streams. Regardless, based on time
spent fishing and lessons learned, I still consider the Rock to be my
home water.

The Rock River wasn't the first river I fished after we moved to the area, but it was soon on my list. Our move took place Thanksgiving weekend. Throughout that first winter, I imagined myself fishing right at home on the Laughing Whitefish. When spring finally sprang and flows mellowed out enough to realistically fish, I was too entrenched in domestic projects to even get out on the water. When I did finally fish, it was on the Laughing Whitefish but not at our property, where the river is not wadable, and tag alders fiercely guard the banks. It was several miles upstream, near the falls. In addition to the Laughing Whitefish, there were a few other trout fishing ventures farther from home, which were all part of our attempt to explore our new neighborhood.

Even though I had not yet fished the Rock, I had scrutinized it for several months as we crossed it each Sunday on our way to and from church. If I remember correctly, I even got out of the car for a better look on a few occasions. The fact that my scrutinizing location was at the edge of the Rock River Canyon Wilderness Area made it even more appealing to me. With all that attention given to it, I didn't wet a fly in the Rock until late September that first season. After several months of anticipation, the experience wasn't exactly what I was hoping for. In fact, it wasn't anything like I had been imagining. Each time I eyed its flow on our way to and from church, my expectations had grown. By the time I actually fished it, what I was envisioning was a magazine-article-quality experience on a blue-ribbon stream.

From previous experience, I knew that brookies would typically be hiding in deeper holes during daylight hours that time of year. So, that's where I focused my efforts. Even the holes, though, were difficult to fish. Overhanging branches, along with sub-surface logs and roots kept the scale tipped in favor of the fish. I did manage to have a few trout encounters, though. There was a feisty little one on my line for just a few seconds before it energetically shook free of the hook. Then, after a few snagged branches, I hooked a larger brookie. Before I could react, it dove under some roots and tangled my line, then got off.

As my time for the day was winding down, I discovered a hole on a sharp bend in the stream. It was ideal from a fish perspective but not necessarily from a fly fishing perspective. Along the outside bank, there was an underwater sandstone ledge that the bend current had undercut. There was a sprawling bush hanging out over the head of the hole and a small tree reaching out over the tail. In between was a variety of other branches and assorted vines that demanded casting finesse and accuracy. I knew the fish had the upper hand.

I could see fish flashing near the bottom of the hole as they dined. My fly turned a fish or two each time it journeyed through, and a couple of trout even followed the fly out to where I could get a decent look at them. It was addictingly frustrating. Every cast felt like it would be the one. The one a trout would actually take. Like any kind of hunting, it always seems like that moment is going to come any second now. There is an anonymous quote that notes that the charm of fishing is that it is a pursuit of that which is elusive but attainable, a perpetual series of occasions for hope. Before the hoped-for moment happened, though, I had to leave in order to get home in time for an important phone call. I thought it was ironic that the call that was pulling me away from brook trout fishing was to discuss a couple of university brook trout studies I had agreed to help with in that same watershed. As much as I was looking forward to the discussion, I still hated to leave a group of actively feeding trout.

What consoled me was the confidence that I would soon be back. I had found someplace close to home that I could call home. Someplace that I could visit often and get to know. For the first time in my life, I had a stream that I felt was *my* home water. Being close to home and easy to get to, my visits have been many. Sometimes catching fish, other times not, depending on the mood of the fish and the fisherman. I often think of the surprise appearance of an eighteen-inch rainbow that darted out from a nearby log pile to chase my fly with reckless abandon as I was casting to an eight-inch brookie. I didn't end up landing that fish, but my memory of the encounter is as vivid today as it was seconds after the hook pulled loose.

As a result of the phone conversation that pulled me away from fishing that day, for a year and a half exploring the Rock River and helping with research projects in an un-named tributary blended together into an endearing study of not only brook trout but the life of a watershed. Part of the reason for my dedication to the research projects was that I was having more close contact with brook trout than I had ever experienced before. The other part was that it gave me the opportunity to steep myself in my home water, which was still a new and enthralling experience for me. I had spent most of my life not having the luxury of true home trout water. Studying and fishing my new home water made me feel like a kid playing in my monster-size backyard. I didn't even want to stop long enough to go back to the house for lunch. The fisheries graduate students, Ben and Jacob, thanked me for helping them every time we were out in the field collecting data. Whether we were measuring and admiring brook trout, swatting mosquitoes, wrestling with uncooperative equipment, or floundering through waist-deep snow in our waders, my reply was the same, "Hey, I've got the best part of this deal. I get to enjoy all the fish and fun adventures without having to write the thesis." And I honestly meant it.

Throughout the research, one of the things that struck me most was how often we found brook trout in places where I didn't expect them to be. It got me wondering why the fish were in what looked like such a vulnerable spot and not more hidden. I was also perplexed as to why we would find numerous trout in one section of the stream and none just a few hundred yards away in a stretch of water that didn't really look any different. It taught me to notice little input seepages and to more closely monitor water temperatures. I tend to think more and to search more thoroughly now when I'm on the water.

For one of my outings on the Rock, I hit my usual stretch of water about 7:30 am, anticipating fish. The first bend hole had several smaller fish flashing down at the bottom of it, which was a touch deeper and murkier than usual. Several casts later, with a tan bead-head nymph, I hooked a seven-inch chub. I moved on. Another chub encounter. I moved on. At one of my favorite holes, even though it too was deeper and murkier than usual, I could see several smaller fish cruising about and one decent size one hanging behind about an eight-inch diameter rock, up against the sandstone ledge that formed the far side of the hole. Numerous casts produced a five-inch brook trout, then what looked like about a fourteen-inch rainbow showed up from against the ledge and took my fly for a ride, but it soon twisted and thrashed enough to throw the hook. Another fifteen minutes of casting produced nothing, so I switched to a red Copper John, which I promptly put in the trees along the far bank. Mumbling, I tied on

40

another fly. An iridescent black nymph. I added a small split shot sinker and started working on getting it to the fish hanging behind the small rock up against the ledge. It seemed like no matter where I cast, the current pulled or pushed the fly away from the ledge and the fish. Close wasn't good enough. The fish didn't budge. Based on its light coloring I assumed the fish was a rainbow. After more experimenting, I finally dropped the fly in the shallow water atop the ledge, just a few feet upstream from the trout. When I teased the fly off the lip of the ledge, it drifted down into what was apparently the feed zone. The foot-long-looking fish popped up and grabbed the nymph on its way by. When I set the hook, I still took it as a rainbow, but after a few laps around the hole, I noticed the white stripe along the leading edge of red-orange lower fins. With its subdued coloring, I assumed it was a female brook trout. I didn't want to stress her too much, so I tried to get her to the net relatively quickly. Apparently too quickly. When she pulled loose from the hook, she was a couple of yards downstream from me. Once free, she settled in right where she was and held there, finning. I didn't want to spook her – as if I hadn't already – so I stood still and just watched. The view was better than a magazine close-up. She probably held there for five minutes. I wasn't sure if she was resting or just taunting me. Finally, she slowly moved up a few feet, then darted to the safety of an undercut in the ledge, right near the rock where the encounter began. I could see her tucked up under the ledge as I moved slightly upstream to cast farther forward in the hole.

I could see a moderate-size fish near the head of the hole. It looked black against a patch of bleached sand. As soon as my fly hit the water, the shadow of a fish was on it. It thrashed through the main area of the hole, scattering several small trout, before I brought the nine-inch brookie into the shallows where I netted it. Away from the light sand, it too was subtly colored like a female. Regardless, brook trout are one of the most beautiful creatures. She wasted no time returning to the depths when I opened my hand. I looked toward the undercut ledge. The larger trout looked back, or at least I assumed it was looking at me. I was sure that every fish in the hole was on to me by that point, so I hooked up my fly and walked away, leaving the larger trout sulking in its cave.

On another cool, overcast September day, I had a couple of hours to invest in my home water while my wife was selling her artwork at the Munising Farmers' and Artisans' Market. From the first bend hole, I coaxed a nine-inch brookie that was sporting his fall colors. The muskrat that I had often seen in that area greeted me, too. It swam out from the sheltered bank with its fur clumped and ruffled, looking like it was having a bed-head hair day, and eyed me suspiciously before ducking underwater. I typically only catch one fish from that hole, but as I was getting ready to move on, I spotted a larger fish of maybe fourteen inches hanging out on the far side of the hole. After a few casts, it moved to the back of the hole, partially beneath a log, where it decided to stay. An overhanging branch kept me from being able to place a fly where it needed to be to reach the fish in that location, so I reluctantly moved on to make sure I had time to fish my favorite hole before needing to go pick up Julie after the market.

At my ledge hole, I caught two small brookies within a few minutes. Then my efforts just turned to casting practice for a while. About an eight-inch trout would dart out from the ledge every few casts to inspect my fly, but a quick look was all I got from that fish. I could also see four nicer fish holding deep up at the head of the hole. Based on flow characteristics and depth, the spot I needed to hit with my fly was nicely protected by a leaf-covered branch. Twice, I got close enough to tick the leaves with my bead-head nymph. Both times, one of the fish moved over to take a look. Both times, I was rejected. In one way, it was aggravating, but then again, somehow it was just enjoyably frustrating.

Looking at the time, I decided the larger fish in the first hole might have moved to a more accessible locale, so I ventured back down there. The fish in question, accompanied by two others that were slightly smaller, was still tucked partially up under the log at the rear of the hole. I tried casting from a few different locations with the same result. Nothing. They apparently knew what was up and were not interested in getting involved. As I watched the largest fish swirl once, I got a good look at how chunky it was. It was a toad. A disinterested toad.

A fine mist was dancing on my face as I watched. Swift, shallow water over a sandstone slab was singing behind me. Satisfied with just seeing more larger trout than I had ever seen before in one fishing venture, I quietly waded toward our Explorer, which was parked along the road, to go help Julie pack up.

Chasing trout in the Rock's familiar waters, some days I feel pretty good about fly fishing, other days I feel hopelessly inept. Sometimes I wonder if I'll ever get there from a fly fishing perspective. Then I think farther back and realize that I felt that way in the early stages of a number of endeavors that I have since become comfortable with. It's reassuring to know that I at least don't have far to go to learn anymore. I finally have home water to fish and learn from.

I didn't fish the Rock the next season until early September. The fact that there was a trail through the deep grass and briars to access the water beyond the thick tag alders near the road didn't give me a good feeling. I know it's a public river and I'm accessing it through public land, but when I see a worn trail and boot tracks along the bank or other evidence of someone else having been there, I can't help but think, "This is my stretch of river. Who else is fishing here? Are they taking care of my river? Are they being reasonable and conservation-minded, or are they hauling out every fish they can?" The downside of a place that is close and easy to access is that I have that mental conversation often.

Once I got in the water above the alders and made it up to the first hole, I was shocked at how much sand had invaded the area. That first hole was nearly gone. I could still see a couple of small fish in the two feet of water that was masquerading as a hole. Being a bit disgusted, I moved on without a cast, only to find the next hole in even worse condition. There was a sand island right in the middle of where the hole used to be. I was amazed at how much my river had changed. Farther upstream, my favorite hole was almost unrecognizable. It was at least half filled with sand. The upper portion was gone, along with the logjam that once guarded it. A sick feeling overtook me.

While I was staring in disbelief, I noticed several fish hugging the bottom. Even though the hole was significantly different, the overhanging branches were not. They were still standing guard. I switched from a dry fly to a hot-belly nymph, which I promptly put in a tree. After rerigging, presentation after presentation the fish held tight, without a hint of interest. Fly after fly produced the same

43

indifference. My sixth fly trial was a red Copper John. After several presentations, a seven-incher near the back of the pack gave it a try and came to my net. I released it, along with the eight-incher that came next. Then I began working on the bigger fish that was next in line. Of course, being the biggest fish, it also occupied the most difficult spot to get a fly to. It was hugging the sandstone wall along the far side of the hole and there was obviously a current reflecting off the wall that kept carrying my fly away from the fish. It wouldn't budge. I watched my fly float past just above it. Nothing. Just to the left. Nothing. After what seemed like an hour, something finally clicked, and it was pulling on the end of my line. It made several short runs before coming to my net. A beautiful brook trout. Based on my hand length, which I know is seven inches, it was easily close to a foot long. A plump, healthy trout. It felt good to wet my hand and gently hold that fish in the flow before it returned home with a flick of its tail. I knew it would have looked good in a skillet, too, but I have a thing for brook trout. To me, they look better in a stream, so that's where I left it, tucked up close to the rock wall.

Taking one last look, I secured the red Copper John to an eyelet and slowly headed downstream. On my way out, I couldn't resist a few casts into what was left of the first hole. The little nymph brought a seven-inch brookie to my net, sporting a sunset autumn glow. I threw a few more casts just because I couldn't help myself. Then I secured my fly again and headed for the truck. The river, my river, had changed significantly, but the trout hadn't. They were still as beautiful as ever.

44

LAUGHING WHITEFISH

Several vehicles were in the Laughing Whitefish Falls parking area when I arrived. Waders and a flannel shirt felt good in the misty late-morning chill. Predictions were calling for sun to break through early in the afternoon, so I quickly assembled the 4-weight fly rod, grabbed my gear, and headed off down the trail. The viewing platform was vacant, so I strung up my rod there to keep my reel out of the dirt. I had my eye on a patch of water just above the falls, sheltered by an overhanging tree. But what fly? That had been my biggest quandary ever since I started fly fishing a few years earlier. I could typically pick out some trouty water but always wrestled with what to tie on the end of my tippet. I picked something with wings that looked a lot like a common housefly for reasons I don't know. After a few clumsy presentations, it dawned on me that if anyone showed up to view the falls, I'd have spectators. The thought wasn't very appealing, so I hooked my fly on an eyelet and headed down the steps toward the bottom of the falls. When I had scoped things out a few days earlier, the water disappearing around the first bend below the falls had looked inviting. Even though it's perfectly legal to fish the river below the falls, I knew the DNR didn't like people climbing over the platform railings. Unfortunately, with the falls plunging into somewhat of a canyon, there's not a good way to access the river right below the falls other than going quite a way downstream and following the river back up. I looked around one more time to make sure nobody was watching and convinced myself that if it was actually illegal to climb over the railing, there would be a sign. Still, I couldn't help feeling a little guilty.

After climbing off the lower viewing platform, I set my sights on a dark run that began under the overhanging branches of a large cedar. I had gotten into the habit of trying to heed the sage advice of spending time watching and contemplating the water before you decide what to do or where to cast. After thoroughly looking things over and planning out a strategy, I made my cast with all the finesse I could muster, gingerly placing my fly on a cedar bough at the top of the run. I quickly glanced at the viewing platform to be sure it was still vacant before doing a short rendition of Yosemite Sam. Then I waded over close enough to use the rod tip to dislodge my fly. As I ventured further downstream, out of sight of the viewing platform, it occurred to me that there's a good reason that many fly fishers pursue the sport as a solitary activity.

It was a pretty stream, but it proved to be more difficult to fish than I imagined. The shallow fast water emerging below the falls continued for probably a few hundred yards. Good holding water was scarce. Or at least that's how it looked to me. There were plenty of rocks and overhanging vegetation. Small side channels weren't uncommon either. This wasn't as easy as I had imagined it to be. So far, there was more frustration than magic. But, still within sight of the falls, I found a short dark run that was at least twice the depth of the surrounding water. It was tucked up against the west bank. There were minor overhanging branches, but the river itself was pretty well open. Still, there wasn't really room to properly cast, at least not for me. After the cedar branch incident, I had switched to a bead-head nymph, so I was able to just swing the fly over to the head of the run without a lot of fanfare.

The first few passes, the nymph hung up on the rocks populating the streambed. Somewhere around the fifth or sixth pass, bouncing the little nymph through the run, the rod tip took a slight bow. I naturally assumed another snagged rock until the line started pulsating, and lively flashes emanated from the tail of the run. The six-inch fish quickly came to hand, and to my surprise, it was a rainbow. At that point in my fly fishing career, I was still under the assumption that most Upper Peninsula streams sported mostly brook trout. A touch of disappointment started setting in over the fact that I hadn't caught a brook trout like I expected. Then I thought, hey, it's a wild trout in a wild stream and I caught it on a fly...this is good. As I looked around, the stream began to show its charm. Of course, the charm was always there. I just wasn't seeing it. As Henry David Thoreau once said, "It's not what you look at that matters, it's what you see." I was still looking at the same river, but I began seeing it differently. Instead of pesky overhanging branches and fly-snagging submerged logs, I began seeing trout haunts and critical habitat.

Things began to brighten, both figuratively and literally, as the sun periodically peeked through the mist and drizzle. Good fishing conditions were waning. I needed to cover more water while I could. The next hour or so brought three more trout like the first one. All six or seven inches. All rainbows. And they all came thrashing from the dark water of a run or hole. I was surprised with each one, still expecting to be catching brookies, icons of Upper Peninsula dark waters. Then I recalled that a few different people had talked of steelhead runs in the Laughing Whitefish. DAH! If steelhead—aka lake run rainbows—were spawning in the river, then of course there would be small rainbows prowling the shadows. It all made sense, but I still wanted to catch a brook trout in what was technically my home water. Home was roughly eight miles north as the crow flies, but crows didn't lay out the roads, so it was roughly a twenty-mile drive to get there. Still, that same river does truly run through the edge of our property, so I considered it part of my home water and I was on a mission to get to know the neighbors, regardless of their markings.

I moved on to what looked like the next stretch of trout holding water. Surely I passed by some other good trout water in my search for what looked like good trout water to me, but I figured that lesson would be for another time. That next obvious trout holding spot came in the form of a deep run formed behind a chute created by a few large rocks. With the tannin water, I couldn't tell how deep it was, but it was much deeper than the surrounding water and it was dark, making it look like a good hiding place. I followed the progression of the nymph with my rod tip until I realized that there was no progression. There were no quivering pulsations in the line, just no progression. *Great*, I thought, *I caught a rock*. Doing my best not to spook any nearby fish, I jiggled and gently tugged in various directions. To my relief, the fly came loose and continued bouncing its way down the run without being intercepted. Again, I tried. Again, I got snagged. Again, I was pardoned as the fly came loose. Again, and again. Snagged, loose, snagged, loose. I knew I should have been using a topwater indicator fly of some kind, with the nymph as a dropper, suspended just off the bottom, but I tended to have an issue with tangling the flies and knotting the dropper line. So, I just dealt with snagging rocks because it was easier than untangling my line after almost every cast.

As I was beginning to think that I must have spooked everything in the run, my line began to dance, and a sleek, silvery form came flashing and thrashing out of the dark. This one was definitely bigger than the rest. Not big, but bigger than the others. It was probably nine or ten inches long. I say probably because it shook the fly loose before I could get it in the net and darted back into dark water. I still counted it as an official catch. Nobody was there to debate the issue.

The sun was showing through the clouds more frequently and the temperature was on the rise. The waders and flannel shirt that were so comfortable earlier in the morning were getting to feel like a burden. Still, I was on a roll. Besides, I hadn't caught a brook trout yet.

I fished a couple of other likely-looking spots that produced only snags. Most of the stream now being drenched in sun certainly wasn't helping either the fishing or my comfort level. So, I decided to fish one last hole. It was a dark bend hole with a pile of logs at the lower end. My hopes were high, but they began to drop with each uneventful pass of the fly. About the time that I mentally gave up hope and just mindlessly tossed the nymph in again for no good reason, God smiled on me one more time and the line began to twitch. As I pulled in the pulsing line, a seven-inch brook trout came thrashing to my feet. It released itself just as I was taking hold of it. On that note, I decided it was a good time to go.

On my way back upstream, I couldn't resist pitching my fly to a nice-looking hole I hadn't noticed earlier because it was tucked in between a couple of downed trees that I had to bypass. On the first pass the hook lodged on the bottom of a submerged log, requiring me to wade in close for a retrieval, no doubt spooking any would-be fly takers. At that, I hooked my fly to an eyelet and continued with my original plan of heading for the truck. That hole was apparently meant for another day.

Several people were on the viewing platform as I headed up the wooden steps. "Get anything?" they asked. "Yeah, a few." It felt good being the guy saying that.

On another Laughing Whitefish venture, it was officially the first day of autumn, so after getting a little work done, I decided to celebrate by taking my fly rod down to the falls later in the afternoon. I say down because the falls are south of my house. According to river terminology though, it's upstream, so I should probably say that I went up to the falls area. Regardless, I fished near the falls.

The parking lot wasn't full, but it still seemed busy, especially for a Tuesday after Labor Day. In the direct sun of the parking lot, the day felt hot. Once I got into the shade of the forest, it was much more bearable. I wanted to fish my way upstream, so instead of accessing the river by way of the viewing platform stairs, I slipped through the woods downstream to a point where tag alders started to dominate streamside vegetation. As I stepped into the river, a fish hit the surface in a minor hole not far downstream. I quietly watched for a bit as I cooled down from my bushwack, but there was no other visible action in the small hole. I snuck down and fished the hole anyway for probably ten minutes, but my fly went unmolested, so I moved on. Fishable water seemed scarce, which is often the case late in the season. The next minor hole was lined with a slightly submerged log on the far side, not far from the bank. Three times I had a trout take my fly near the log. Three times the fish shook loose within a few seconds. The final take was on the far side of the log after I watched the fish take a real bug there. It was hooked good enough to quickly pull it over the log but again shook off the hook before I could get it to my net. After that episode, the fish were obviously wise to the guy with the long stick in his hand.

I found one other good-looking hole prior to reaching the falls, but a tiny sapling hanging over the water intercepted my fly. Retrieving it spooked everything in the hole. It only looked like a few small fish, but as a matter of principle I was still miffed that I had snagged the tree, even though it was right where I needed to place my fly.

I did exploratory casts to several other places before reaching the falls, mostly just because I was fishing, and I wanted to fish. Twice while exploring, I got snagged and in the process of popping the fly loose, I somehow managed to tangle my tippet to the point where I couldn't even tell how to untangle it. The second tangle included a portion of my leader and was intense enough that I almost gave up and just cut the line to start over. After a few minutes of fussing with it though, it all of a sudden came undone without me having any idea how. I just said thank you.

The final fishable water I found was right at the base of the falls, out in front of the viewing platform. Fortunately, nobody was there viewing. As I approached, I saw a fish slowly disappear into a small logjam to my left. There was no good way to fish near the logs, so I focused on the main run coming out from the falls. Right away I hooked a fish but just as quickly lost it. A couple more unsuccessful quick hits later, I finally netted a brightly colored male brookie of about nine inches. It boasted prime fall colors. After a couple of quick wet photos, I turned it loose. It slowly cruised between my feet, then darted to the safety of the logjam.

Several casts later, after a couple of unsuccessful hits, I netted an eight-inch rainbow. As I was trying to take a one-handed picture of it in my net, it shook loose and slipped out of the braided enclosure. Several more casts produced a few more quick hits, then the run went quiet, or at least the fish did. I took a few pictures of the falls from my prime vantage point in the middle of the river, then began climbing the stairs to the top of the falls with a spring in my step. Even though I had only landed a few fish, I had technically caught several. Autumn was off to a good start, at least in my world, and local streams were becoming more familiar with each cast. A trip to real trout water could be measured in minutes instead of hours, which meant that I could realistically fish for trout pretty much any day that I wanted to. From a fishing standpoint, I could get downright spoiled if I wasn't careful. On my way back to the truck, I thought about whether I wanted to be careful or not.

LITTLE GARLIC

My introduction to the Little Garlic River was a random decision to fish the upper reaches near the main falls. It was our first year of being true U.P. residents, so pretty much everything in the area was new and interesting. Why the Little Garlic Falls area had specifically caught my interest, I don't recall, but we made plans and went. We, being me and my wife, Julie. As an artist, Julie wanted to do some plein air painting – painting outdoors, on location – and collect reference photographs for later painting in her studio. I simply wanted to fish someplace new.

The parking area for the falls was about three miles down Little Garlic Road, where the road crosses its namesake river. I took the empty parking lot as a good sign that we at least wouldn't have a crowd to deal with. Based on fresh tracks in the mud, a bear had apparently recently crossed the bridge, coming over to the side that we were on. I took that as a positive thing because it added to the sense of adventure. Julie didn't comment. According to the trailhead sign, it was just over a mile to the falls. For some reason that must have made sense at the time, I decided to go look at the falls first, before I carried in my fishing gear. I have since wised up. To my credit, it only took that one time to learn my lesson, which is unusual for me. It typically takes me two or three tries.

A couple hundred yards into the hike, we heard some brush breaking and caught a glimpse of a black furry rump retreating through the forest underbrush. We didn't hear anything splashing across the river, so the rump owner must not have gone far. After listening intently for a few minutes, we quietly continued on, not knowing if the smallish rump belonged to a young adult bear or a cub – there's a big difference from a safety standpoint. The remaining twenty-minute hike was thankfully just a quiet stroll through the woods.

The falls were only about eight feet tall, with a hundred yards of mixed cascades and pocket water below. Moving water danced in sunbeams streaking through openings in the forest canopy. There were chutes and runs and holes, white water, gravel, boulders, and bedrock. There were quiet woods and stone guardians that hosted emerald green moss and orange lichens. It looked like a fitting home for wild Northwoods trout. At the lower end of the cascading stretch there was a rustic campsite, complete with a rickety latrine. That's where I started my fishing venture – the campsite, not the latrine. It was already mid-afternoon because we had to hike back to the truck to get the fishing and painting gear after we conducted our initial evaluation. I made a mental note not to make that mistake again.

As I rigged up my rod, there was no hesitation as to which fly to start with, a red Copper John. I had heard that brook trout love red, so what else could I use if I wanted to catch brook trout? The nymph bounced its way through a run that was tight against the far bank right in front of the campsite. Actually, it only made it about halfway through the run before it snagged on what I assumed was one of the many rock slabs that covered the riverbed. I managed to free it without much fuss or fanfare. The second pass through the run provoked a hard strike that ended as quickly as it had happened. I reached behind me to make sure my net was in place and ready to go. The next, much more excited cast resulted in a major snag. None of the non-invasive techniques seemed to make any progress in dislodging the fly from its hold. At that point, I'm sure that I muttered something, but I don't recall exactly what. I finally resorted to running the rod tip all the way down to the fly in an effort to free it. After fussing around and spooking anything that was in the run, I came up with an empty leader.

I tied on a new tippet and a twin to the #14 red Copper John that I had just lost. I also decided to venture farther upstream, where I found a small hole with an overhanging stump. My fly snagged on some unseen object on the first pass. Second pass. Third pass. After four or five snags in a row – I was too busy mumbling to count – I decided to move on again. The next promising-looking hole was situated where I knew that I could not get into a reasonable casting location. To spare myself the frustration and loss of another fly, I moved on without a cast. Having Julie painting off on her own worked out well because that meant that there were no witnesses to my fishing escapades. At least I had that consolation going for me.

The next few fishy spots produced nothing but a temporary hooking of a two-incher. Technically, it was a trout, but technically, I didn't actually land it either. So, I was still fishing zero. Maybe a change of flies. A #14 Pheasant Tail nymph caught my eye, so I tied it on. Finally, in a small section of pocket water, between two small chutes, I legitimately caught a trout. It wasn't the brook trout that I was hoping and fishing for. It was a rainbow. The UP was supposed to be a brook trout stronghold. Maybe I didn't catch a brook trout because I took off the red Copper John. I consoled myself with the fact that it was at least a trout, hooked through the lip on a wild stretch of river. A wild trout at that. All four inches of it. I wasn't skunked for the day. Even though it wasn't a "keeper", I wasn't planning to keep it anyway.

Before I made it upstream to where Julie was painting, I had another four-inch rainbow in hand. Not that it mattered, but the second fish might have even been pushing five inches. Then I realized that both fish measured together still didn't make a legal-length fish. Too much thinking. I needed to get back to fishing.

A somewhat tenuous bushwack around a vertical rock outcrop brought me to where Julie was painting. It turned out that her painting was going about like my fishing. In fact, she didn't have any evidence either because she had covered her painting with a coat of white so she could start over. I decided we would both be better off if I didn't get involved, so I turned my attention to fishing a small hole, fed by a fast-water chute right in front of me. The first dozen or so passes produced nothing but minor snags. I probably should have just called it good at that point, but Julie didn't look ready to leave yet, even though she wasn't actually painting anymore. We were in a beautiful location, in no rush to leave, so I continued fishing. A few casts later, the 4-weight rod bent slightly, and my fly came back sporting a six-inch rainbow. Being my biggest fish of the day, I had Julie take a picture of me holding it in the water – she wasn't really doing anything anyway. As I was releasing my fish, it occurred to me that with a combined measurement, I had caught a respectable rainbow, more or less.

Watching the sun's evening rays sparkle off the falls and the bubbling cascade above, I realized that this experience was playing out just like my first local UP fishing venture on the Laughing Whitefish. Below the falls, I was catching rainbows. I ventured a guess that above the falls, otherwise known as a barrier, I would likely find brookies. My guess included some brookies below the falls, too. I just hadn't caught them yet. I considered bushwhacking my way around the falls to try to find out, but that's when I noticed Julie packing up to leave. The sun was steadily sinking, and my stomach was starting to grumble about neglect. Proving my theory would have to wait for another opportunity.

As Julie shot a few last pictures of the river and falls bathed in fleeting sunlight, a mink darted past and disappeared into a mossy rock crevice. We left it alone and quietly began our twenty-minute stroll through the evening forest.

The following year, I returned to the Little Garlic, intent on fishing my way through the Trout Unlimited, Elliott Donnelley Wilderness that was downstream of the falls area. My wife and I had recently hiked a majority of the wilderness trail that naturally followed the river. From our vantage point atop the ravine that guided the river, we had seen numerous holes and deep runs that looked inviting to fish.

While perched along the top of the ravine, I had made a mental note to get back there and actually fish those holes and runs before the regular trout season ended. So it was that I found myself standing on the riverbank, just beyond the wilderness access parking lot, scrutinizing the river for likely trout-holding water. With water levels being a little low, even for early September, I knew my best bets would be those deeper holes and runs that had previously caught my attention.

As I slowly worked my way upstream into the ravine, I soon came to realize that most of those deep-looking features were actually only eight inches of water running across a dark section of sandstone bedrock. Most of the rest of the water was only about six inches deep, at best. Regardless, the river and surrounding scenery were beautiful, and I assumed the fish would be beautiful as well if I could only find them.

About halfway through the day, I finally found a legitimate hole with a small collection of rocks scattered across the bottom. From what I could readily see, which was pretty much everything, the hole contained two trout. One looked to be about seven inches long and the other about five inches. On that clear, sunny day, both were about as wired as a couple of ADHD kindergarteners on a sugar buzz. Needless to say, I didn't catch either of them. I did manage to pull a six-incher out of the next somewhat hole a little farther upstream and another small one from the hole above that. There was also a large log lying parallel to the bank, with some deeper water around it. We had eyed it from above during our hike, and concluded that it was a definite fish home. Maybe even an apartment complex. The only thing I ended up coaxing out of it was a muskrat. Fortunately, I didn't accidentally hook it. I had read about incidents like that and was happy not to be able to write about it myself.

At the last hole of the day, I ended up fishing it from the three-foot-high bank because that was the only place that I could fish from without spooking the entire hole. A big log with several branch remnants spanned the river near the back of the hole, adding to the access issues. As is often the case, the front of the hole was guarded by some overhanging tag alders, as was most of both sides. From up on the bank, I could see a lone trout, which I was sure was a rainbow, cruising the scene. Periodically, the fish would hold in one location for a short time, apparently evaluating the situation. Its length looked like it might be at least close to the ten-inch limit for a legal rainbow. Certainly not big but at least worth trying to catch. If nothing else, just to see if I could.

I probably spent at least forty minutes on that quest, with a #14 Hotbelly Nymph. In hindsight, I should have switched to a general-purpose dry fly, like a stimulator or an Adams, partway through the exercise, but I didn't. At one point, as I was holding the fly suspended above the water while pondering my next move, a big dragonfly kept attacking my fly. Even though it was interesting, I wasn't there to catch dragonflies. The fish did come after my fly a couple of times, but each time, it changed its mind at the last second, or something changed, whether there was cognitive thinking involved or not. Twice I got snagged, and of course popping the fly loose from the snag resulted in the line wrapping around my rod numerous times. Once, while I was untangling the line, I looked up to see "my fish" just upstream from me, in an easy place to cast to. I was convinced it was taunting me, probably giving me a fishy smirk.

Eventually, with a cast and drift that I didn't perceive as being any different than numerous others, the trout darted over and matter-of-factly snatched my fly. I had to scramble down the three-foot drop-off to land it, which I managed to do almost gracefully – meaning I didn't fall in. Being feisty as rainbows often are, the fish made one water-spraying leap two-feet into the air, before coming to my net. I didn't bother with a formal measurement. I simply admired the wild rainbow for a few seconds, then opened my hand and set it free, satisfied that I could indeed catch it. Having experienced a personal brush with the wild was equally satisfying. After taking a deep breath of north woods air that was beginning to carry the taste of autumn, I broke down my rod and packed up my gear.

Just downstream was a sloping ridge that led to the top of the ravine. I followed it up to the trail. Looking back over the river below, I realized that the hole I had just successfully fished was one that I had been excited about during our recent hike. Maybe things were coming together a little better than I realized. On that thought, I began a slow stroll out of the wilderness, just to savor the day – and to keep from overheating. The only fish I carried were in my head, which was fine. If the rainbow had been sizeable enough to feed both me and my wife, we would have been enjoying it for dinner. But I was satisfied with the realization that days like that one feed more than just your stomach.

THE YELLOW DOG

My introduction to the Yellow Dog River was one of those spur-of-the-moment visits to a place that I previously didn't even know existed. My wife and I were spending a few days in Big Bay, in Michigan's Upper Peninsula, to celebrate our fifteenth wedding anniversary. It's hard for me to believe it was more than twenty years ago that we spent that long weekend at the Big Bay Lighthouse Bed & Breakfast. As with most excursions like that, our days consisted of leisurely exploring the surrounding area. One of those explorations included Hills Falls (or Yellow Dog Falls as some people refer to them), which is now part of the Yellow Dog Watershed Preserve. Somehow in that relatively brief visit, something about the Yellow Dog connected with me. I wasn't sure what or why, but there was a definite bond. I had a feeling that our flows would cross again. I hadn't started fly fishing at that point, but I've always had a fascination for moving water. I didn't know anything about the river's origin, its history, or the tragic source of its name, but for some unknown reason, I was enamored with its flow.

Roughly ten years later, when I began dabbling with fly fishing, I would think about the Yellow Dog now and then as I was planning outings and making mental lists of where I wanted to fish. Being that it was a good nine-hour drive from my home at that time, and I would have had to pass numerous other trout streams during the trip, I never made the venture.

After my wife and I moved to the Upper Peninsula a few years ago, fishing the Yellow Dog was moved up higher on my list of things to do. Still, there were plenty of other activities and opportunities vying for my time, including a good selection of unexplored trout water that was closer to home.

When I did finally manage to fish the Yellow Dog, a couple of years after we became locals, the excursion just ended up being an afternoon of wetting some flies while practicing my casting. Of course, not being familiar with any other stretches of the river, I fished between County Road 510 and the falls, on the Yellow Dog Watershed Preserve, which sees quite a bit of foot traffic and fishing pressure, so my lack of success shouldn't have been a total surprise. I had explored the main pool below the falls, as well as a couple of runs extending out from the pool, using a dry fly and two different nymphs. I believe I started with a Copper John, then switched to a different nymph, but I don't recall exactly which one. I eventually changed to a dry fly, just because the nymphs weren't bringing any success. In hindsight, I probably should have started with the dry fly before probing the depths, but hindsight, as always, kicked in a bit too late. Besides the falls, I did fish a few other sections of river on the way back to my truck, but at that point, my expectations had already dropped to the point where it may have been affecting the outcome.

More recently, during a conversation with Jim Jenkin, a Trout Unlimited buddy of mine, we got to talking about how we needed to do some fishing together. The conversation ended with me and Jim deciding to amble up to the Yellow Dog. He had fished a stretch above county road 510 after we finished our Partners for Watershed Restoration (PWR) Brook Trout Committee project tours a two weeks earlier. The Brook Trout Committee is a group of organizations, individuals, and government agencies interested in making things better for brook trout in the western Upper Peninsula, and we had been looking at potential restoration projects, including several that would positively impact the Yellow Dog watershed. Jim had done well on his Yellow Dog excursion, meaning that he caught a number of fish and simply had an enjoyable time on the water. That sounded good to me. In fact, just getting in a river with a rod in my hand sounded good to me—my waders had been dry for way too long for no other reason than my priorities had been out of whack. Catching a fish or two in the process would be a bonus more than a requirement.

Jim and I started near the mouth of a small feeder creek where we had investigated a potential restoration project, and worked our way upstream, playing leapfrog. Jim gave me the first stretch, which included a large mid-stream boulder and a collection of overhanging branches along the far bank. I was fishing a yellow stimulator that Jim had tied. He said that fly was what he was using on his previous successful visit, which sounded like a good reason to at least give it a try. Besides, there weren't any hatches in progress, and I liked the versatility that the stimulator could be fished on the surface as a dry fly or pulled under and saturated for use as a wet fly. A couple of false casts later, it could be aired out and floating on the surface again. I didn't manage to find any fish hanging out around the boulder, but the yellow stimulator did readily bring a couple of seven-inch brook trout out from under the branches to take it from the surface, which was a promising start to our fishing venture. For some reason, though, everything felt awkward, like when you've got a bad head cold and it feels like your brain is about two steps behind your body. I was functioning like I hadn't been out in a while, which as I said, I hadn't. The fluidness of my casting was like spring break-up, where sometimes the water's flowing and other times it's still a little stiff. I didn't leave my new fly in a tree, though, so I considered it somewhat of a successful start.

A short distance upstream was a deep, well-guarded, bend hole, fed by fast water through a dead-fall gauntlet. It was one of those areas that obviously held fish but had a good selection of features for holding flies as well. I looked it over but decided to bypass that area to keep my fly and my confidence intact. Jim wasn't much farther upstream, so I did my first leapfrog around him. When he asked how

I did, I mentioned the two fish but kept the other comments and feelings to myself. I think he and I both knew he was a better fly fisher than me. I figured there was no need to elaborate on it.

Upstream, I coaxed a couple of eight-inch brook trout from a dark run coming out of a heavily wooded bend hole. It reminded me that one of the simple blessings of trout fishing is sensing their innocent wildness pulsing at the end of my line, then opening my hand and watching them return to the river. Afterward, I dabbled a bit in the bend hole but knew I was flirting with losing a fly, so I left it at a flirt and moved on, feeling a little more like an actual fisherman than just someone who was out fishing. There was plenty of wood in the river. In fact, some areas were literally a wooden fortress. Periodic stretches of overhanging tag alders added to the fish cover, though the stretches of tag alder were typically short. The challenge, at least for me, is figuring out which areas of fish-holding, woody cover I can get a fly into and out of as opposed to just into. Some days my perception is better than others.

Farther upstream, I found several fishy-looking runs and holes. Most produced a trout or two. I didn't land them all, but at least I felt the thrill of the tug and saw the flash of the take in the water. Most of the fish I hooked were in the eight-inch range. One that was inhabiting the shade and shelter of a large overhanging maple was ten inches. All brook trout. The ones that didn't come to the net simply thrashed around enough to throw the hook. I suppose there may have been a time or two when I just didn't set the hook well enough or quickly enough. Sometimes there's a fine line between setting the hook and pulling the fly out of the fish's mouth.

I lost my first yellow stimulator on a back-cast bush. I heard a slight rustling of leaves behind me as I was moving into my forward cast, but it was too late to react. My flyless tippet came forward and landed gently on the water. It would've been a nice presentation if it had had a fly on it. A five-minute search turned up nothing but leaves. The evening was waning, so I tied my last yellow stimulator on and got back to fishing. I figured somebody would probably find my liberated fly come fall when the camouflaging leaves were gone.

The long hole I was fishing at the time was bordered by a tall bank on the far side. The bank was beginning to cave in here and there, which left some woody obstacles along the water's edge. After several casts, I hooked what looked like a brookie of around twelve inches for a few seconds, until its highly animated thrashing popped my 7x tippet. My suspicion was that the tippet had somehow been damaged previously, but it didn't really matter at that point. I was out of yellow stimulators, so I tied a Mickey Finn to the end of a new section of tippet to see what I could entice with a streamer. About my tenth cast, I went a little long and the Finn was intercepted by a scraggly finger of a branch on the remaining two feet of what was once a spruce tree.

With the water too fast and deep to wade across, I tried reaching with the rod tip to push the fly free. It's a technique that I've used often. It just didn't work. In my continued frustrated attempts to free the streamer, again, my tippet gave way and left the hapless Mickey Finn dangling from the scraggly finger.

As I was mentally debating my options, I glanced at my watch. It was pushing 9 pm, which was a few hours past normal dinner time. My stomach was beginning to comment about that. As I looked around, Jim was coming upstream to meet me. He had news of similar results but with fewer fly losses. After our brief pow-wow, we agreed it was time to call it an evening. We didn't have any new tales of big fish or exotic adventures, but after the fun of catching and releasing several feisty brook trout, we were both content that our time on the water was another evening well spent.

Walking the gravel road through the forest back to Jim's vehicle, it felt like something was missing. Then I realized that mosquitoes were almost non-existent, which was a pleasant surprise for late July. The lack of their constant hum and harassment allowed my mind to wander. As we walked, I thought back to our tour of potential Yellow Dog conservation projects a few weeks earlier. Somewhere in the mix of those discussions, I had overheard Jim asking Yellow Dog Watershed Preserve Board President, Chauncey Moran, where he grew up. With a smile, Chauncey replied through his bushy white beard, "I haven't grown up anywhere, yet."

The wisdom of that reply kept scrolling through my brain. In some ways, we should all hope to not grow up. To not lose our youthful sense of wonder and adventure. To never quit dreaming of things that ignite our imagination and keep us ever excited about the possibilities of tomorrow. That's one of the benefits of trout fishing, particularly fly fishing for trout. It's a youthful quest. There's always more to learn, not only about the art of fishing, but about trout and where they live, and everything that makes up that environment. There are always things to be excited about and look forward to. There are always adventures to be found in moving water, whether you're fishing and exploring an un-named hop-across-width creek or a major blue-ribbon trout stream.

The Yellow Dog is probably somewhere in the middle of those extremes. Even though it's much more than a small creek, the Yellow Dog certainly isn't considered to be a blue-ribbon trout stream either. In fact, I've heard some people refer to it as *marginal*, as far as trout water goes. As is the case with most Michigan rivers, the Yellow Dog suffered its share of abuse during the logging of the area's virgin timber, but most of those wounds have long since healed. It still has its scars and blemishes for sure, as most of us do. For instance, some of its tributaries contain perched culverts that need replacing, and there are a few stretches where sandy banks are eroding and caving in. There's some mining in the area that people are keeping an eye on, and a few tracts of private land where the owners don't necessarily have the best conservation practices in mind. Although they're not good, those situations don't tarnish the river's appeal in my mind.

The fact that the Yellow Dog originates within the nearly-seventeen-thousand-acre McCormick Wilderness and that it empties into Lake Superior are endearing qualities to start with. Knowing that there was a time when it was known as The River Where Yellow Dog Was Killed, because of a massacre that occurred near its mouth, also adds a bit of wild mystique, even though it has nothing to do with the quality of fishing—blue-ribbon or not.

I don't usually search out and fish blue-ribbon trout streams anyway. Not that I have anything against blue-ribbon streams. In many cases, those streams just require more extensive travel than I typically invest in a day of fishing. They also tend to be fanfare destinations that include blue-ribbon dining and blue-ribbon lodging, which are typically above my means. Those streams are certainly aesthetically appealing and tend to be prolific trout producers. They also serve an important role in concentrating fishing pressure in a few key waters, leaving most other streams more open for people like me. Part of my aversion to those high-profile streams may just be because I'm not exactly a blue-ribbon fly fisher, so in a way, maybe I have a subconscious concern that blue-ribbon trout are more educated and sophisticated than my abilities can handle. I like to think that it's simply because blue-ribbon streams are usually busier and more crowded than I like, so I tend to gravitate toward less glamorous water.

I say less glamorous not meaning anything denigrating about the streams. I'm simply referring to streams that don't necessarily have high popularity rankings amongst trout fishing circles because they're not known for high densities of large fish. That term also applies to streams whose names you're not apt to find peppered throughout popular fishing literature. Mentioning their names won't likely silence nearby conversations and turn heads to casually eavesdrop on your discussion.

Popularity aside, the Yellow Dog is more than just a river. More than a watershed even. It's water and soil, gravel and rocks for certain; a vast collection of trees, grasses, wildflowers, moss, and lichens; it's the interdependence of creatures like deer, bears, moose, fishers, squirrels and mice; the blending of songbirds, bald eagles, hawks, and owls; it's local people living close to the land and water; distant people yearning for reconnection; lives of all kinds intertwined with its flow. On a cool morning, with a faint mist rising from the murmuring water, herbal scents of the forest drifting on invisible currents, and the soothing sounds of a living landscape greeting the day, it's a present glimpse of the beginning of time. When life was a matter of simply living. When industry and urbanization, competition and greed, even monetary value, had not yet even become distant thoughts. Like many rivers, the Yellow Dog is a connector, binding what appears to be individual and separate pieces into the whole of life. It's a community.

I envision that if every river was part of a community, and every community was blessed to be part of a river, maybe happiness and contentment wouldn't seem so difficult to attain. Maybe there wouldn't be so much turmoil in the world. Everyone would understand the importance of caring for our land and water. Resources would be more appreciated and less exploited. There would be more bonding and fewer battles. Life may not be any easier, but it would probably be a little less complicated. We wouldn't need to travel to the river to unwind and sort things out. We'd already be there.

Looking back on our evening on the river, one of the blessings of a community like the Yellow Dog is that even if you don't actually live within its geographic footprint, you can still be a part of it and feel like you belong. With community, comes connection and commitment. It's not a formal requirement. It just naturally happens. In my case, things were just a little out of order and the connection came first, years before I even realized what I was connecting with. Now that our flows have more thoroughly intermingled, community and commitment are finally settling into place.

I can't say that I would call any of that marginal. You could readily call it engaging, enriching, or maybe even enchanting. Fulfilling comes to mind, too. But most people simply call it The Yellow Dog.

UNEXPECTED ENCOUNTERS

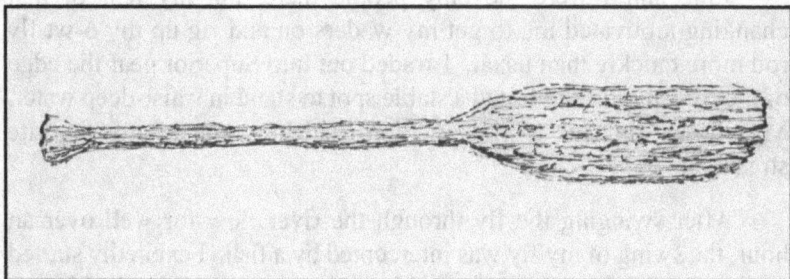

T he roughly two-mile hike out to the mouth of the Montreal River in the Keweenaw Peninsula wasn't anything out of the ordinary, except for the fact that I was wearing a large canoe pack, loaded with my waders, fishing gear, food, water, and an odd assortment of other things that I had deemed necessary for our explorational venture. My intention was to fish the plume where Montreal Falls tumbles into Lake Superior. I had never fished there before, but being mid-May, my understanding was that the list of potential catches included coaster brook trout, steelhead, and splake. I had told my wife, Julie, that I would consider catching any of those fish to be a success. The honest truth was that it sounded like a cool place to fish and catching anything would be considered a success.

When we got there, part of me just wanted to dink around in the falls, which is typical of me. More of me wanted to ignore the scenery and rush straight into fishing. It felt like an exotic place to fish, with the roaring falls spilling into the expanse of Superior. As much as I wanted to just relax and enjoy the experience, the anticipation of what might be waiting out there to be caught was churning inside as much as the falls were churning outside. I didn't want to miss out on any of the experience even though I knew that just being there was part of the experience. I finally decided that the best way to calm down and engage in the moment was to become an active participant and get in the water so I could start fishing.

Julie and I were the only people there, but my fear of that changing motivated me to get my waders on and rig up my 6-wt fly rod more quickly than usual. I waded out into Superior near the edge of the river plume and found a stable spot to stand in waist-deep water. My chosen fly was a Mickey Finn, which is one of my favorite streamers.

After swinging the fly through the river flow for well over an hour, the swing of my fly was intercepted by a fish. I excitedly started reeling the fish in as I began working my way toward shore. Playing a decent-size fish and wading across a rocky cobble shoreline should probably be two separate actions. I mistakenly combined them into one. About halfway to shore, the fish made a hard run as I stumbled over a loose rock, which resulted in the fish pulling free from the hook.

It's a depressing feeling when the line goes slack after an incident like that. I just stood there for a moment in thigh-deep water, thinking of things I should have done differently. The one short glimpse I had of the fish, just before its freeing run, had me estimating its length at about twenty inches. The glimpse hadn't been enough to recognize any markings, so I had no idea exactly what I had lost other than it was a nice fish and it looked trouty.

I shook off the depressing thoughts by telling myself that I had at least hooked into a nice fish in a beautiful location and that there were likely more out there navigating the flow. Then I somewhat optimistically worked my way back out to about where I had been before and started the rhythmic cast and swing routine again.

After what felt like at least another hour of no fish breaking my rhythm, I noticed a guy coming in on the trail. From the corner of my eye, I could see him standing there watching me. In my peripheral vision, he looked like a normal guy. I had nothing against him. He probably simply wanted to fish, just like me. It was just that at that moment, the merging of river and lake, that particular mixing of water in that snippet of time, was my world and I didn't want to share it. Assuming he wanted to fish where I was fishing, I avoided making direct eye contact for fear that direct eye contact acknowledgment could be misunderstood as an invitation to join me. Instead, I kept fishing, and he meandered up along the falls, dabbling around like I was initially inclined to do.

Feeling a little relieved, I went back into my fly-swinging routine but soon realized that Julie was hanging around near our packs, so she was probably done taking pictures of the falls and surrounding scenery. I had promised to quit fishing in time for us to take a look at the upper falls before we needed to head back to our car. I had to remind myself that the fishing was an add-on to a day of exploring the tip of the Keweenaw, which was part of a few days of general Keweenaw exploring. I could tell that Julie was killing time, waiting for me to make good on my promise. I could either start packing up my gear and preparing to move on to other explorations while we were both still in a good mood, or not. As bad as I wanted to continue fishing until I actually caught and landed a fish, from an overall trip perspective, *not* didn't seem like the best option.

As I made my way out of the water, there was a slight emptiness in my stomach. It's a feeling I often have when I'm in the process of ending a hunting or fishing outing. I always feel like I'm going to be missing something when I leave. Making the decision to leave is tough. Once the decision is made, a feeling sets in that's a lot like regret. Maybe remorse is a better word. I don't really want to go, but I know that I should, so I do. Once I took off my waders and physically started packing, the feeling faded, as it usually does. Some beef jerky and a handful of Cheez-Its helped.

Having accepted the fact that we were leaving the lower falls, I felt inclined to be more neighborly, so I found the guy who was still tinkering in the falls and let him know I had vacated the prime fishing spot. He thanked me and headed that way, trying not to look like he was in a hurry to get there.

After we finished our snacks and packing, Julie and I hiked the short distance to the upper falls, while I checked out the river for our next — hopefully longer — visit. On our way back through by the river mouth, I saw that the guy I had ceded my fishing rights to was netting a fish. Curiosity made me casually stroll down for a quick look.

JOHN HIGHLEN

He had a nice fish of about eleven inches and was trying to decide if it was a coaster or a splake-coaster mix. He told me that a fisheries biology professor at Michigan Tech was convinced that splake were interbreeding with coasters, diluting their bloodline. I had to admit, it was a tough call. The fish in his hand had the markings of a brook trout, but the end of its tail wasn't as straight as I would expect. It didn't really have the slight "V" indent of a splake either. It was a pretty fish. We just couldn't confidently determine exactly what it was.

As my new friend slipped the stocky fish back into Superior, right near the falls, he said that it didn't really matter to him, as long as there were healthy, lively fish to catch. He didn't offer up his name. I didn't ask. It didn't seem important. We had a conversation about fish—brook trout, lake trout, splake, and steelhead to be specific. That's what was important. We seemed to share a fondness for wild brook trout—catching them, releasing them, and having them around for the future. That was important, too. I think we were both honestly happy for each other's fishing adventures on that gorgeous Keweenaw afternoon as well. That, too, was important. The experience and the meaningful conversation we would remember. Names, we likely would not. So, we simply wished each other well, and I think we both sincerely meant it. Then I strolled away toward an evening campfire, and he went back to focusing on floating imitation spawn through churning water in the hope of another brush with the mystery of a wild trout.

During our hike to the trailhead, my mind drifted back to the fish conversation. Brook trout versus splake versus crossbreeding of a crossbreed—was it a coaster or the diluted offspring of a coaster? My new friend seemed happy with either, as long as there was a good fishery to experience and enjoy. Of course, the definition of what a good fishery actually is can become a topic of debate. Would I hate to see coaster brook trout disappear? Absolutely. Maybe. I'm not sure if I would even know that it happened without some scientist or wildlife professional telling me. If I was still able to explore and play in clean, wild lakes and streams, chasing wild trout, would it really matter? I don't know. I can't say that I ever experienced a coaster before. I thought I saw one once as I peered into calm Superior water off the east break wall in Grand Marais, Minnesota. But, then again, maybe it was a splake.

In a similar vein, do I care that wild grayling no longer exist in Michigan? Yes, because it was the result of environmental decline and greedy, senseless slaughter. Has it affected my life? Not that I know of, but then again, maybe it has, and I just don't realize it. Regardless, not knowing the possible consequences, why not lean to the conservative side and work to keep from losing any more species? Why not take steps to help keep coaster brook trout around? It certainly can't hurt. If we wait too long for too many studies, it just might be too late.

Even after rethinking things by a campfire that evening, my thoughts didn't change, so I naturally assumed that they must be good thoughts.

On the way home from our tip-of-the-Keweenaw visit, there was another, much less cordial encounter. With the thought of coasters swimming through my head, I decided to stop and fish the Pilgrim River near Houghton. The Pilgrim is known to still support a population of coasters, so I wanted to at least familiarize myself with it even though I knew that we didn't have a lot of time available that day. We would be driving right past it anyway.

For my introductory fishing excursion, I worked my way upstream through part of the Pilgrim River Community Forest, more exploring than fishing. After enjoying a snack while sitting on a mid-stream boulder, I made my way toward an inviting-looking bend hole that was just upstream. As I slowly approached, I noticed another fisherman on the wooded high bank above the hole—high, meaning at least fifty feet. He obviously wanted to fish that hole—presumably he had had success there before—because as soon as he saw me, he charged down the steep wooded bank toward the river, lost his footing and subsequently his balance. His less-than-graceful descent came to a crashing halt, partially in and partially out of the water, just upstream from the hole. As he clamored to his feet, he slung a splashy cast into the center of the prime fish-holding water. As I stood there watching his performance, the guy fired two more casts that sounded like he was throwing baseball-size rocks into the water.

At that point, he was apparently either convinced there was nothing there to catch or satisfied that there was now nothing there for me to catch. After a quick glance and sheepish nod in my direction, he moved on upstream.

At first, I was ticked off and seriously considered yelling something at the guy, but I couldn't help laughing at his pathetic antics, which quickly diffused my anger. After standing there for a few minutes, chilling in the flow of a north woods trout stream, I decided to let go of that encounter and headed off in search of Julie.

In some cases, people encounters are not even with the people themselves. My friend Jim Jenkin had extended a last-minute invitation to go fishing on part of the Escanaba River watershed. With the regular trout season soon coming to a close, I readily accepted the invitation. The Middle Branch of the Escanaba was bigger water than I typically fished, but I quickly came to appreciate having room to cast properly. From the middle of the river, I could readily cast to both banks and any features in between, without worrying about getting snagged on my back cast.

I spent an hour or so swinging a Mickey Finn streamer through every place that I thought might be holding a trout and a lot of other places in between those places. I did well—casting that is. Fishing was non-existent. Well, that's not really true. Fishing was great. It was the catching that was non-existent.

As I began working my way back upstream to where I first entered the river, I kicked something with my right boot. Looking down through knee-deep tannin water, I saw the ghosted form of a canoe paddle somehow lodged on the river bottom. I wondered what was holding it in place as I used the toe of my boot to lift the handle up enough that I could reach down and grab it. The waterlogged paddle was gray with age and exposure. The protective coating of varnish was gone, along with a significant portion of the outer layers of wood, leaving the paddle heavily textured and fragile. Holding it in my hands brought to mind a weathered pair of oars that I found years ago at the bottom of the Grand Canyon, stashed in a jumble of boulders along the Colorado River. In the case of the oars, being that they were tucked away together indicated that they were purposely put there. Even though when and why were unknown, the story behind the oars didn't tug at my imagination like the old paddle I was holding.

I stood there in the river, wondering how old the paddle was and where it came from. Who lost it? Did its story include the long-ago capsizing of a canoe, or was it simply accidentally dropped into the flow? I knew there was a story. There always is. I just didn't know if the paddle's story was interesting and adventuresome or simply a mundane mishap. Being that I'm not a big fan of mundane things, I naturally assumed that it was an interesting adventure that brought the old, worn paddle into my hands that September afternoon.

Standing there in the late afternoon glow of Fall colors, admiring my new old paddle, I took a deep breath of autumn air, then headed off to show Jim my catch.

Not all interesting encounters are with people, or even have anything to do with people. Fish can unexpectedly squirm their way into your life sometimes, too. At times, even masses of them can take you by surprise. We were camped at Fort Wilkins State Park, near Copper Harbor. It was our mid-May, pre-summer-chaos camping trip. It's usually the last time we can really relax before the summer craziness begins. We had witnessed a run of suckers in Fanny Hooe Creek before, but it was nothing that I would consider writing about. During a daytime excursion, I had noticed quite a few suckers in the creek, with more gathering in the shallows near the mouth. That night, as our campfire died out, I casually suggested to Julie that we should take a headlamp hike over to the creek to check up on the run.

As we approached the creek, the night air smelled like a fish house. The usual mingled scents of north woods pines and vast fresh water were completely overpowered by the strong smell of fish. When we cleared the trees and our headlamp beams illuminated the creek, what we saw was a creek of suckers that were stacked up to the point where the backs of the top layer of fish were sticking out of the water. It was like that from the first cascading falls, down to the mouth and out into the shallows of the harbor.

In a relatively narrow band of open water along the creek bank, our headlamp beams occasionally highlighted a brook trout—typically seven or eight inches long—apparently trying to avoid the mayhem that was consuming the rest of the creek. I was tempted to run back to camp and grab my fly rod to see if the brookies would take a fly, but I decided that they had enough stress in their lives at that moment. They didn't need me adding to their issues.

It was difficult to pull myself away from the chaotic drama of the creek and turn my headlight beam toward camp. Even once we finally did, there was a burning temptation to return to the intermingling of water, suckers, brook trout, and darkness. But it was getting late. The sensible thing to do was to clean up and sink into a cozy sleeping bag.

Thirty minutes later, I was laying there in my cozy sleeping bag, looking up at the tent roof, thinking that I should have stepped quietly into the edge of the creek with my headlamp off, carefully eased my hand into the water, and waited to see if the fish would eventually accept me as a threatless part of their environment and brush against my hand. I don't know how long it took, but I finally drifted off to sleep, wondering what was going on at the creek and wishing that I hadn't been so sensible.

Next time, I'll step into the ensuing drama to make it a physical encounter, instead of just watching and wondering, "What if…"

DOWN SOUTH

Everything I had heard about Cooks Run, in the Iron River neighborhood, made me want to fish it. We had had plans to do just that for a couple of weeks, but weather and other things kept getting in the way. The day that Bob, Steve, and I finally made the drive south, we began our search at Dark Water Outfitters and Fly Shop. Seth Waters, the owner, wasn't there at the time, but we found a friend in another local who was sipping on a cup of Joe in the coffee shop in the front of the building. Burt had helped build some brush bundles on a slow, wide stretch of Cooks Run that our TU Chapter had sponsored. So, even though the three of us from up north had never actually met him, we were more or less friends from a trout perspective.

His directions to *The Meadows* were a little rocky but easy to follow. At the end of the two-track that Burt had told us about, we found a slow-moving stream winding its way through a mix of tall grasses and tag alders in an expansive bog. The brush bundle project was to narrow the channel, increase the current, and trap some of the spring-flow sediment. From the evidence that we saw, the project appeared to be working well.

As Bob and I stood on the bank contemplating what we wanted to do, a fish – presumably a brookie – took a bug from the surface at the edge of a shadow near the opposite bank. It looked like it had some size to it; the fish that is. I wasn't sure about the bug. It was late morning, and the sun was distancing itself from the horizon. As a result, the shadow across from us was getting to be a rarity. Without much for cover, the fish would be getting pretty spooky in the sunlit water. Steve returned from his foray upstream, reporting we would need extra-tall waders to venture very far. It was tempting to rig up and give it a try, but there was already a vehicle parked near the stream when we arrived. It had out-of-state plates and a fly rod leaning against the back hatch. The driver and possible passengers were nowhere to be seen. With no idea of who or how many fishers were already there or which direction they went, we decided to bounce our way back out to the main road and try another location. On a Monday morning, the good fishing spots shouldn't all be occupied. Hopefully, the stream wasn't *that* popular.

The second access point Burt had mentioned was an old train trestle. We readily found an old train trestle, but for some reason, we weren't quite sure it was the train trestle Burt was talking about. The water was clear and running at a good trout speed. Shade and cover were abundant, but the promise of an even better option drove us onward. Shortly after moving on, a little more scrutiny of the map showed that the trestle we had seen was indeed the trestle we were looking for, but having already passed it, we found another road crossing nearby on the map and decided to take a look at Cooks Run there.

We easily found the crossing, but the sign introducing it as the South Branch of the Paint River threw us off a bit until we looked closer at the map and noticed its junction with Cooks Run just upstream. The river at hand was a pretty stretch of water with several text-book trout-holding features within sight. Being that we were already there, and morning was quickly ticking into afternoon, we decided the name of the river didn't really matter. We were pretty sure the brook trout didn't care, either. So, we strung up rods and pulled on our rubber pants, although they're not actually made of rubber anymore, but that didn't matter either.

I stepped in on the upstream side of the bridge because Steve stepped in on the downstream side. Bob opted to study some maps to better understand the area and to figure out where we were with respect to where we had installed some temperature loggers during our previous non-fishing visit. I had my eye on a shadowy outside bend that was protected by overhanging brush. The red #14 Copper John made several passes past, and even underneath, the brush fingers unmolested, so I decided to put it just a little closer to the bank, where I could envision brook trout lying in wait for hapless invertebrates tumbling by. That's when the branches did what branches do and intercepted my Copper John on its way to the trout. No amount of flicking, twitching, or verbal rebuking seemed to improve the situation. So, I reluctantly waded over to retrieve the fly. I didn't actually see any trout fleeing my intrusion, but I was sure they did.

Then I turned my attention upstream a few yards to where a chute between two boulders created a relatively swift, deep run that tailed out right behind me. I positioned myself where I could drop the fly in at the head of the run and follow the drift all the way down to the tail-out. After several uneventful drifts through the run, my line started dancing, and a feisty seven-inch brookie came to the net. Even though brilliant spawning colors were still at least a couple of months away, it was still an incredibly beautiful fish. Maybe that's part of why I have a thing for brook trout. They're just beautiful creatures. As I quickly pulled it from the net and returned it to the current, with a flick of its tail, it was gone, back into the shelter of the dark run. Several casts later, I was admiring another similar size brookie. That one came from the tail of the run, after the fly was beyond a natural drift and beginning to sweep across the current. A few minutes later, a third brook trout emerged from the run, again striking as the nymph started the cross-current swing. That one was an eight-incher. Technically a keeper if I was inclined to take it home for dinner. It rejoined the others, and likely more, back in the shelter of the swift run.

I felt good about the fact that my casting was improving considerably. I was finally letting the rod do its job instead of trying to muscle the cast. Fly fishing was becoming much more relaxing, yet it was somehow intensifying my concentration and focus. I knew I still had plenty to learn, but I finally started feeling like a fly fisher as opposed to looking and feeling like some schmuck standing in the water waving a rod around. I was also beginning to pick apart the river, noticing seams and holding areas. Even though I still wasn't reliably putting the fly exactly where I wanted it every time, I was closing in on the mark. I did still have work to do in learning to read the current to know where to place the fly for the drift I wanted, but like with most things, there always seems to be something to work on.

The big question that I came away pondering was whether seven- and eight-inch fish were all that there were where I was fishing or were they just the biggest ones my current skill level could fool. I suspected that it might be a little of both but mostly the latter. I also began understanding where the seven-inch brook trout size limit on most streams came from. That appeared to be about where the number of fish you can readily catch starts seriously tapering off, making catching a limit of fish more difficult. Maybe it's based on something more biologically scientific than that, but it sounded like a good theory to me. Besides, I wasn't inclined to keep any brookies anyway, so it didn't matter. Not that I consider killing a brook trout a mortal sin or anything. I just don't like killing them. Even though I know that a good share of Upper Peninsula brookies can probably be traced back to a stocking truck somewhere in their lineage, in my mind they're natives. I don't doubt that at some point I'll eat a brook trout or two, but the circumstances will have to be just right. That day, though, the circumstances leaned in favor of the fish. I let them return to their normal lives, content in knowing that they were still out there. Even though I know that brook trout are plentiful in UP waters, I like doing my part to ensure they don't somehow share the fate of Michigan grayling and passenger pigeons. I have friends who regularly tell me they're delicious. I certainly don't doubt the truth of their convictions. Still, when I decide to enjoy eating some trout, it'll likely be non-native rainbows or browns.

After a few casts to the smoother water above the chute, I saw Steve wading back toward the bridge. A glance at my watch said that

I should, too. The popular adage says to take nothing but pictures and leave nothing but footprints. I skipped the pictures that day and just took some memories with me. Although, closing my eyes, I realize that I do have some pictures in the mix.

During another southward trek, we spent several hours building more brush bundles along the banks of Cooks Run in order to narrow the stream, which increased the water velocity to help scour out silt deposits that had been forming due to the wider stream and slower flow. This was part of a multi-year project in conjunction with the Forest Service to help the stream recover from degradation that resulted from past logging practices and other human tinkering.

After completing the brush bundle work for the day, my friend Mike Golas invited me to join him in his canoe for a little Cooks Run fishing. We spent a couple of hours working our way upstream from the project area, through a section of the stream that slowly meandered through what looked like a meadow of tall grass with some mixed brush. Being that I had the luxury of having a seasoned local in the stern seat, I didn't need to concern myself with where we were or where we were going. I could just fish. Having never fly fished from a canoe before, casting from the bow seat felt a little awkward at first, but I eventually got the feel for it enough to catch a small brook trout on a parachute Adams. The fact that I didn't end up hooking myself or Mike during my canoe-casting introduction was a pleasant success, too. We eventually got out of the boat to do some casting near an old beaver dam. Sometimes beaver dams improve fishing opportunities, sometimes they don't. The only way to tell is to try it. As I recall, Mike caught a couple of brookies above the dam and I caught one just below the old structure. Mike was fishing with a tan bead-headed nymph, so I tried switching to a few different nymphs in hopes of catching a few more fish. It sounded like a good idea, but it ended up not paying off in terms of additional fish. Overall, the dam structure didn't seem to improve or degrade the fishing. At least it didn't for us. Regardless, the fishing itself and experiencing an area that was new to me were the main successes anyway. Catching a couple of fish while honing my casting skills from a canoe was an added bonus.

I've been told that there is no shortage of good places to fish for trout down in the southern portion of the UP. I would have already tried more of them by now if it weren't for the fact that there is no shortage of good places to fish for trout all over the Upper Peninsula. So, for now, most of those good places to fish are still on my to-fish list because I've been busy fishing other good places to fish. It's an enjoyable problem I suspect will carry me through the rest of my days. If not, I guess I'll just have to buy a Wisconsin fishing license and start a new to-fish list.

BACK HOME

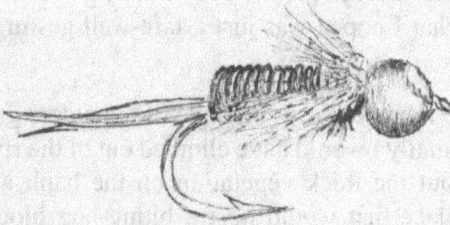

On a mild summer day, after wrapping up some responsibilities, I decided to responsibly go fishing. It had been a while, and I didn't want it to turn into a long while. With part of the day already gone, I also didn't want a long drive. So, I left home to visit my home water. The fishing there was certainly not as good as it was prior to the influx of sand the previous year, but it was still my close-to-home, comfortable place to dance with trout. My new routine was to simply make a few casts into each remnant of a hole while I was enroute to the only real hole remaining in that particular stretch of river. I didn't really expect to catch anything with my ceremonial casts. It just seemed like something I should do. Maybe, in a way, I was paying homage to the river that once was.

At the second remnant, my first cast brought a quick hit-and-run strike that snapped me out of my autopilot daze. The second cast brought an eight-inch brook trout to my net. The awakening felt refreshing, like a cold sip of your favorite soda during a hypnotizingly familiar drive. Even though we may have met before, I think the trout and I were both surprised to see each other. The hook was in good, but I managed to quickly remove it without any real damage. It was the same sharp hook that got my finger three times while I was rigging up. At least on those occasions, the barb didn't go in. I turned the brookie loose in what I hoped was just a fare-well gesture and not a true goodbye.

Up around the next bend was a tangle of tag alders guarding the river channel. Normally I would have climbed out of the river and by-passed that area, but the thick vegetation on the bank and beyond looked like someplace that would host a biting-bug block party. I opted to fight my way through the overhanging alder gauntlet. My net got entangled once, but I managed to come out the other side of the hazing with my equipment intact, and without drawing blood.

When I reached the only true remaining hole, there were a number of little fish jockeying for position in the trailing edge. Beyond that, the water was too murky for any sightings. An assortment of overhanging branches in front, and a tall mixture of bank vegetation behind me left short roll-casts as my only real option. A few casts into my exploration, a nice trout of about twelve inches rose up from the murk to investigate my fly. My pulse picked up noticeably. Several times I saw that fish take at least a passing glance at my offering. Then, a slightly smaller trout darted in and snagged my fly. Before I could set the hook, it was off again. Another trout, a little smaller yet, then took its turn at my fly but quickly threw the hook as well. Several casts later, each full of anticipation, a nine-inch brookie was trying its strength against my 7x tippet. The tippet won, but I opted not to claim my prize. It darted back to safety as aggressively as it had hit the fly.

Then came the usual we're-on-to-you lull. I swapped the yellow stimulator for an elk-hair caddis, and the dances resumed. I again had what looked like a ten-inch fish on for a few seconds. The twelve-inch trout made a couple more investigations, too. An eight-incher made a quick hit-and-run without getting hooked. Then another lull. I forget what the third fly was, but it was another medium-sized dry fly. Before I cast the new fly, I watched, hoping for a hint for what to do next. My hint came in the form of a faint glimpse of the twelve-inch fish hugging the bottom at the edge of the hole, just inside the edge of visibility. It was facing the flow coming in from the side, where the river made a sharp ninety-degree turn. I cast into shallower water in front of where I had glimpsed the premonition of a fish. As my fly drifted toward the edge of the hole, slightly below the surface, I watched the trout slowly rise from the bottom, right into the path of my fly. When the fly was about to bump it on the nose, the trout matter-of-factly opened its mouth and the fly floated in. The trout closed its mouth and sank back toward the bottom. As I excitedly lifted my rod to set the hook, the fish turned toward me and the fly popped harmlessly out of its mouth. It swirled and disappeared for the last time.

At that point, I should have just accepted the loss. The fish was on to me anyway. Adrenalin was doing the thinking, though, so I swapped to a light-colored bead-head nymph, with no success other than a few fry poking at it. A red-brown wooly bugger brought a few curious bumps from small trout, but that was it. My final fly was a Micky Finn streamer. All it brought were a few casual follows by a six- or seven-incher. After a number of completely fruitless casts, I finally accepted the obvious fact that the inhabitants of the hole were wise to what was going on. The music was off and the dance was over, so I did the equivalent of putting away the chairs by clipping off my fly and hanging it on my drying patch.

As I stood there near the edge of the dance floor, thinking things over, a blue heron popped in over the trees but quickly banked to the south when it spotted me. I quietly made my way toward the truck. As usual, I wasn't bringing any fish home with me, but I had experienced the magic with every investigation, swirl, and almost catch. I had wetted my net and it smelled like fish. There were five flies on my drying patch. All had been bitten, except for one. And there was a nymph drying in a tag alder across the river. I left with a good collection of visions in my head and a little more experience under my belt. It was a good day to be hanging around home.

One late August day, I spent the last few hours of daylight at that last remaining hole of my home water go-to stretch. The tag alder security force ate up a little more of my evening than I had hoped. Against my wishful thinking, the sand had not miraculously disappeared, either. The murky, sluggish-looking water looked like August. I had tied on a dry fly before I left the truck, but with alders hanging over the hole even more than usual, there was no room to cast. Not even a decent roll-cast. So, I switched to a weighted nymph, which allowed me to basically just flick the fly into place, or at the very least, I could resort to a cane pole swing. The first several passes – notice I didn't say casts – produced a couple of quick hit-and-runs, just as a tease. Then the action went dead. Well, there was still plenty of action with fish flashing as they fed down in the murkiness. The action just didn't involve my fly.

I switched to a different nymph. Same thing. The sun had already set, and the evening chill-down was in progress when I finally got a legitimate take. The tugging at the end of my line was a gratifying feeling after a summer sparse on fishing. A shiny rainbow of about ten inches came writhing to my net. I thought about keeping it as I said a little thank-you prayer. It was tough to get an exact measurement, though, as the fish was squirming in the net. It was close to the legal ten-inch limit, but I just couldn't tell for sure if the last eighth of an inch was there or not. If you have to discuss things with a Conservation Officer, the last eighth of an inch is as important as the first, so I pulled the net away and let the fish slide from my hand. It was gone before the tail cleared my fingers.

I made several more casts, but the word was apparently out. Fish continued flashing in the dim light but ignored my fly altogether. I quietly reeled in, hooked up my fly, and waded downstream in the evening calm. At the tag alder gauntlet, I opted to get out and bushwack. It was hard to decide if I made the right choice or not. Regardless, I made it out to the truck, a little warm, but with no loss of blood. Instead of breaking down my rod, I wove it through the back seat and up onto the dash, hoping for a few casts at the next river crossing. Below the old train trestle, I cast a couple of different flies, but nothing came out of the black water. It did feel refreshing to actually be able to cast, though. With darkness creeping in, I decided I had better wade back across to the trail while I could still barely discern the river bottom. I reached the road as a soft mist was rising from the swampy area to the south. I stood for a few minutes, soaking in the evening. Then I unseated my reel, broke down my rod, and nodded farewell to the river.

Late autumn, well after regular trout season, I had spent a brisk November day hunting for deer in the wilderness area that my home river flows through. As I waded back across Silver Creek on my way to the truck, and again at the road where Rock River crosses, I thought of fishing. Normally I don't think about fishing much in November because I'm too absorbed in searching for deer, but on that particular evening, fishing memories swirled through my head. Standing on the bridge over the river in the fading evening light, dressed for deer hunting, I was transported back for a moment to the Platte River. Sometimes my dad and I would fish for coho in the afternoon while we were camping and hunting in the area. Dad's been gone for a long time now, but sometimes moments like that bring stray memories up from the depths. In a way, I missed my past life. Then again, I realized that I like where I'm at now. Having grown kids that are doing well, and grandkids to play with is a good place in life to be. Having *Home Water* and being able to have wilderness adventures close to home, is a good place in life to be, too, even if things are a little murky sometimes.

TROUT DREAMS

When we first moved to our UP home, I was mesmerized by all the little creeks that crossed our property. Some are ephemeral, simply transporting extra snow-melt water. Others are year-round waterways that eventually feed into the Laughing Whitefish River at the back of the property. I highly doubted that any of our creeks supported fish, due to the fact that they all filtered through a cedar swamp on their way to the river, but to a person who had never owned property that contained a real stream, I was enthralled. On our downstate farm, we did technically have a creek, but it simply connected two swamps and had been converted to a farmland ditch by a prison work crew many years ago, when prison crews did that sort of thing. Here at our new place, my expectation was that I would be exploring and delighting in our newly acquired miniature rivers for the rest of my days, even if it didn't involve a fly rod.

I tend to get caught up in moving water. It's been that way for as long as I can remember. Well before I ever even started dreaming of fly fishing. Moving water just pulls me in—sometimes figuratively, sometimes literally—whether it's a major river or a trickle in a ditch doesn't necessarily matter. The current gets inside my head and gets my thoughts flowing, too.

Late winter, when weather fluctuations begin to foretell times soon to come when streams run in earnest and a green tinge begins sneaking through the woods, led by a parade of trout lilies, always catches my attention. That's when I especially start dreaming trout dreams, putting aside snowshoes and cross-country skis. Those passing transition seasons are like markers, showing us that time relentlessly marches on. At this point in my life, though, the march feels more like a trot. And the trot gives me sore muscles. I'm trying not to think about the fact that the march of time will soon feel like a long-distance run. Moving water helps keep my attention off those thoughts.

I like taking walks during the winter-spring transition. Anytime the road or trail crosses a stream, I linger. Those narrow channels of open water that first appear, offering tantalizing glimpses of life and movement, get me thinking about trout. Particularly brook trout. They begin haunting my thoughts. That mental dance continues until the opening of trout season. At that point, in one way things get better because I can get out and fish. In another way, the hauntings get worse, because I can get out and fish. Same thing happens with deer season.

For me, trout dreams come in many forms. One of my dreams has long been to catch a big brook trout. Of course, *big* is a relative term. Early in my trout fishing quest, a big brook trout was about ten inches. That was when the biggest one I had caught was roughly eight inches. Now, I consider a big brook trout to be at least fourteen inches. That's because I have now caught brook trout close to that size. Like with most goals, each time I catch a bigger fish the definition of big goes up accordingly. It's part of the dark side of human nature. We always seem to strive for something beyond what we have already obtained – or attained.

Fishing with a good bamboo fly rod is another dream that has been rattling around in my skull for a while. Not that a bamboo rod helps you catch more fish. It's the look and feel of a bamboo rod. I have heard it's like the difference between paddling a wood or wood and canvas canoe compared to one of the newer synthetic designs. It's in the feel and handling. Not that I have ever experienced a wood or wood and canvas canoe either. I just want to feel the difference for myself. I imagine it to be like comparing the ride of a Mercedes with the feel and handling of my model-year 2000 F250 pick-up. The truck gets me where I need to go – when it starts. With well-worn shocks and considerable play in the steering wheel, the handling isn't what most people would call world-class. It has developed a few squeaks and rattles, but those are usually overcome by radio volume. Bumpy roads are the biggest issue. That's where I need to continually monitor my mirrors, keeping an eye out for rusty parts lying in the road behind me. I couldn't care less about owning a Mercedes. It would just be interesting to feel the difference. Same goes with a vintage canoe or a quality bamboo rod. It would just be nice to have the experience sometime. Then again, if a bamboo rod turns out to be too much of a great experience, I might start seriously conniving how to acquire one. Same goes for a vintage canoe. Both could turn out to be costly scenarios. Maybe I should just leave those both in the realm of dreams and invest the money in a truck.

Catching a wild grayling has long been a dream of mine, too. Maybe it's because they were once abundant here in my home state and now they're not. Or maybe it's because of their unique character, with that shimmering iridescence and sail-like dorsal fin. Regardless, there is something about them that I like, and I would love to catch one. I tried chasing grayling once, in Glacier National Park. I didn't win the fishing grand prize, but the consolation prize was a nice rainbow that certainly tasted great cooked over our campfire that evening.

Another one of my early trout dreams was the fabled AuSable River. I had ogled the legendary river at seventy miles per hour for years as I crossed its flow enroute to and from other northern destinations. Not being a fly fisher in those days, I never stopped to get acquainted. Once I started down the fly fishing road, I initially still didn't fish the AuSable because I was at least a little intimidated by its popularity and reputation. After gaining a tiny bit of experience, meaning I could cast a fly without completely embarrassing myself, I ventured up to Gates Lodge on the legendary stream. Once I arrived, I realized tinges of intimidation still lingered, so I eased into things by aimlessly looking around the fly shop first and buying a few of the flies they recommended. Then, I decided I needed to have lunch in the lodge's dining room. I remember the food being good, but I have no recollection of what I ordered. At the time, I was absorbed in staring out the big windows at the river.

Not knowing what else to do, I eventually rigged up my rod and carefully stepped into the river in front of the lodge. The thought of asking someone in the fly shop for a suggestion of where to fish did cross my mind, but I didn't want to look like a complete idiot. In hindsight, flogging the water right in front of the lodge probably wasn't the best alternative.

I did manage to eventually calm down, allowing me to throw some decent casts. At least I thought they were decent. Apparently, the fish didn't agree. During the couple of hours of working my way downstream through a section of what is known as The Holy Water, the PhD-level trout chose not to engage with the elementary-level fisherman in their midst. Even though I didn't catch any fish that afternoon, just the experience of fishing a portion of the AuSable made me feel more like a fly fisher. If anyone asked, I just didn't elaborate on the details.

My second AuSable outing again involved Gates Lodge. The difference was that I enlisted the half-day services of a guide. That difference made a big difference. Mark was an experienced fly fisher, quite a few years my senior. He was relaxed and knew how to work with someone who wasn't. After a session of lawn casting, he took me up to the North Branch to chase brook trout. To my surprise, within ten minutes of arriving, I caught one. It looked to be barely legal length, but we were not keeping any fish anyway. That success, as is usually the case, set the tone for the rest of the morning. Even though my casting abilities were still on the low side of adequate, I caught a few beautiful brookies and gained some experience I had long been dreaming of.

I returned to the North Branch one more time to extend my original adventure there. That time, my wife, Julie, accompanied me. We spent two days at Fuller's North Branch Outing Club, in Lovells. It was the late side of early September, right between what some would call prime trout season and upland bird hunting season. We pretty much had the big historic lodge to ourselves, except for a lone gentleman whom we only saw for a brief introduction.

Julie and I hooked up with our guide, Cameron, at about 9:00 am, and he introduced us to a quiet stretch of river about a fifteen-minute drive from the lodge. A few blue-winged olives were coming off the water, causing an occasional fish to rise. Being Julie's first time fly fishing, she did well. At least well enough to catch the first brook trout of the day. A healthy eight-incher. I soon followed suit with a similar fish. Then a breeze picked up, the sparse olive hatch came to a halt, and the trout went on break. We eventually caught a few more trout by switching to streamers. They were obviously beginning the transition to their fall spawning colors. Trees were beginning their fall color transition, too, but they still didn't compare to the radiance of the brookies. They're definitely spectacles worth dreaming about.

I was going to say that I had lots of trout dreams when I was a kid. Now that I think of it, though, I still have lots of trout dreams – and I haven't been mistaken for a kid in a long time. The truth is, now that I know more about life and fishing and have experienced more of both, I have lots of dreams for all sorts of outdoors ramblings – and other ventures, too, for that matter. Some dreams have even made it onto paper in the form of rough plans. I have found that when I start estimating costs, that's where most rough plans abruptly terminate. Still, I keep the notes around in case circumstances change.

Sometimes, trout-related dreams simply come in the form of mental ramblings. Sitting near the mouth of Sable Creek, resting on a logjam log, sunlight was dancing with the creek. Over, under, around, or through obstacles. They danced. I thought of how the stream carries whatever comes to it, good or bad. It does not differentiate. It cares not. Sand, trees, fish, gravel, people, trash, it just does the work of moving whatever comes to it as it wanders to its place of rest. I thought of that a few days later, as I was peering into the Laughing Whitefish River from the M-28 bridge. The river does not depend on fish or other creatures. It's just hydrology in action. It's physics. Water falling to a place of rest. It doesn't depend on fish or aquatic insects or trees or people to survive. Rivers and streams are in their simplest sense, just moving water. They're transporters. Fish, though, depend on the river, on water. All living things depend on water, depend on rivers and streams of all sizes to live. The river just does what it does. The burden, then, is on us to work with the river to accomplish the business of living. The living of fish, animals, trees, and people alike. The river just keeps flowing, or at least tries to. It does the work of moving. We do the work of living. We and every living thing in and around the river. We're together in this dance of life.

Another form of trout dreaming that I often indulge myself in is keeping a list of streams I want to fish. Some are realistic. Others will likely never leave the realm of dreams. Then again, sometimes the only thing separating a dream from an experience is a plan. There have been numerous incidents where I dreamed of doing something for a relatively long time, then when I finally planned and did it, it turned out not to be nearly as difficult, time consuming, or expensive as I expected. Of course, there have also been times where when I finally do something after a long stretch of serious dreaming, it doesn't turn out anything like I envisioned. Agate Falls is a good example of that. We had been crossing Agate Falls at sixty-five miles per hour for probably twenty years as we traveled to and from Minnesota and Wisconsin destinations. The name alone had grabbed my attention and made me want to fish there. Finally, my friend Doug Miller and I made rough plans to do it. Two years later, our plan came together, and we actually set a date for an Agate Falls fishing venture. It was a beautiful autumn day on a gorgeous stretch of river. We had the river to ourselves most of the time we were there, allowing us to fish when and where we wanted to at our own pace. Doug caught several fish. In fact, he caught a UP trifecta of trout—brook, brown, and rainbow—and shared his successful fly pattern with me. Everything aligned with my dreams and expectations except for one detail. In all my mental adventures, I caught lots of fish, including some big fish. In the reality version, I didn't catch squat. I did see one small trout and a pair of coho, but nothing even touched my hook except for a tree and two logs. Okay, three logs. Sometimes, it does take a few tries to get reality and the dream to match. Of course, I've noticed that when I'm dreaming or daydreaming about trout, I usually fish better than I do on the water. That's when I'm mentally living the lives of another John, like Gierach or Voelker.

It often doesn't take much to get the dreaming started, regardless of the type of dreaming we're talking about. I have even spawned a few trout dreams while gazing at lethargic fish cruising the somewhat natural-looking waterways at Cabela's. Shortly afterward, I usually find myself admiring the store's offering of new fly rods. Then I go home and start recording the mental lists that are developing in my head. Fortunately, there isn't a Cabela's in the Upper Peninsula. That saves me a considerable amount of money.

Even without artificial dream sources, here in the UP there is no lack of rivers, streams, and creeks to get the process started. Flowing water just seems to carry adventurous thoughts and waters dreams to make them grow. The fun thing about dreams is that they are unlimited. Time and money, on the other hand, are not. Still, dreams help us through dry times and often end up shaping reality. Fortunately, chasing the magic doesn't necessarily require a lot of money, and the magic isn't always tied to far-off lands or exotic locations. Even though dreams do often travel far and wide, chasing the magic associated with those dreams can be as near as you need it to be.

HURRICANE

My wife, Julie, and I were spending a few late September days camped at the Hurricane River Campground in the Pictured Rocks National Lakeshore. Besides enjoying some autumn evenings by the campfire and exploring the area without wasted travel time each day, I wanted to explore the lower reaches of the Hurricane River with a fly rod. Just above the first bend, barely two hundred yards from Lake Superior, is a cascading waterfall that I had been admiring for a couple of years. Besides the scenery and atmosphere of the falls themselves, I had been eyeing the pool below the falls as a fishing acquaintance that I would like to make.

As we were roaming around on the first evening of our stay, I spent some time in the hemlock shadows on a high bank overlooking the pool. A large fish was cruising the pool, momentarily silhouetted against the light features of a relatively shallow sandbar, before fading back into the darkness of the deep. Several times I saw the fish cross a section of light sand before I noticed differences. I was watching multiple large fish. At least three as far as I could tell. They looked like steelhead, but that was mostly a guess.

While I was watching, three fish attempted the falls, black silhouettes amidst white foaming water. One fish made it to the top and beyond. The other two were washed back into the darkness of the pool. About the time I decided to walk back to camp to get my fly rod, a fisherman with a spinning rod came stalking down the trail. As soon as he noticed that I didn't have a rod with me, he wasted no time in descending the steep bank and sneaking out onto the edge of the sandbar. Using weighted imitation spawn made from orange yarn, he began methodically drifting the imitation meal through the hole and on through the adjoining dark run.

I stood back and watched, curious to see if he managed to catch anything. After about twenty minutes of fishing, he left with a nice steelhead and a small coho. Even though I was a bit jealous, I was mostly irritated with myself for not just bringing my fly rod with me to the river in the first place. As daylight faded, I saw two more fish attempt the falls, both barely making it a quarter of the way up before retreating to the shelter of the hole below. I ambled back to camp, scheming for the next day.

First thing the next morning, I was standing on the edge of the sandbar, right where the guy from the previous evening had been. My orange yarn imitation of spawn made numerous trips through the falls' plunge pool and adjoining run with nothing to show for it. Not even a tentative bump or hit. After more than an hour, all I managed to do was lose two flies to unknown snags. It looked so easy when the other guy was doing it, so I couldn't help thinking that I must be doing something wrong.

Julie had told me before I left camp that she wanted to go kayaking on Grand Sable Lake. Even though she was willing to wait until I was done fishing, I was feeling a bit disgusted with how things were going for me, so I sulked back to camp and traded my rod for a paddle.

Evening found me back at the Hurricane River falls pool. Same plan. Same fly. Same results. I couldn't believe it! Nothing. Again. With every drift, I visualized a fish taking the bait. Steelhead? Coho? I didn't care at that point. What was I doing wrong? Was I using enough weight? Was my drift realistic? Questions without answers rattled through my head as I spent another night by the campfire thinking through my fishing and lack of catching.

Most of the next day was taken up by a commitment to have a booth at Agri-Palooza, which is an outdoors and agriculture-related event for area fifth graders. Throughout the rainy morning and into the drizzly afternoon I talked to the kids about coldwater conservation and trout, wrapping up with a fly-casting session. As I was standing in the rain making presentations and casting to grass, my brain kept wanting to drift back to a dark hole at the base of a cascading waterfall.

Mid-afternoon, the event ended, and I packed my gear and soggy butt into our Explorer and headed back to camp. The elastic at the bottom of my rain jacket had been pulling the back of the jacket tight across the seat of my pants, directing a half day's worth of rainwater there as well. On my way back to camp, I had to sit on one of my other previously dry jackets to keep our Explorer seat from getting soaked.

By the time I reached Hurricane River Campground, raindrops had given way to a generally soggy, blah afternoon. The thought of putting wet pants into waders wasn't exactly appealing, but not having brought a lot of extra clothes, I didn't want to change clothes just because they were wet either. As a compromise of sorts, we decided to take a dry-out walk out to the AuSable Point Lighthouse before I engaged in evening fishing. With the seat of my pants still being wet (including long underwear, underwear, and a folded bandana in each pocket), at the beginning of our hike, it felt like I was wearing a wet diaper. Julie said that I walked like it, too. I ignored the comment and kept waddling along.

By the time we returned to camp from our roughly three-mile hike, I was fairly well dried out and warmed up. At least enough to be able to put on my waders without it feeling disgusting. Fishing with yarn spawn hadn't panned out, so regardless of what worked for the other guy, I tied on a streamer. Within thirty minutes, I hooked six fish: four for just a few seconds, one for a short tussle until it did a tail-walk across the water and threw the hook, and one that I successfully landed. I say successfully because I actually had my hands on the small steelhead for a short time. It had apparently slashed at my fly as it swirled and got hooked in the side of the head. As I was removing the hook, it thrashed violently, breaking the tippet at the fly and escaping my hold. A few seconds later, it was gone. During my thirty minutes of glory, I had also watched as a fish of about twenty inches followed my fly across the edge of the sandbar until it spotted me standing about ten feet away. In the end, all the fish were again hiding somewhere in the dark and I was standing on an empty sandbar.

Another thirty minutes of fishing and two fly changes later, I hadn't experienced anything except a wet fly. Even though we obviously were not having fish, I decided it was a good time for dinner back at camp. On my way to camp, I lingered on the high bank overlooking a logjam just downstream from where I had been fishing. A few fish were milling around near the logjam, in a place I didn't think I could successfully reach with a fly. As I was thinking that this is probably where fish from the falls hole go to when they get spooked, the fish sporting my recently lost streamer swam out from the cover of the logs. I suspected that the rest of the fish I had been fishing for near the falls were also mingling with the logs below me, which would explain the sudden end to the action. I continued on my way back to camp, enlightened.

Early the next morning, I was back at the falls pool. On my way past the logjam, I stopped for a few minutes to watch the gathering of fish. Being in a well-protected location that was difficult to fish, I didn't even give it a try. Numerous fly losses and frustration were a given, so I continued on to the falls. After thirty minutes of fishless casting and retrieves, I conceded that the fish were likely all hiding in the logjam fortress downstream. There was no telling when some would venture back up to the plunge pool. I could either wait or indulge Julie's desire for a long hike on our way home. We left the trailhead at Kingston Lake an hour later. In my head, I carried a few Hurricane River lessons: If something isn't working, try something different; If the fish are not biting, maybe they're not there; If you're not finding success, try again later; Enjoy the scenery, even if it's fishless.

A few weeks later, we stopped at the Hurricane River on a sunny autumn day for a quick look on our way to pick up Julie's artwork from a nearby gallery that was closing for the season. Several fish, presumably salmon, were gathered below the falls. After visualizing fishing for them for a few minutes, we went on our way, leaving the fish and the river to continue with their day as well.

Since that time, I didn't fish the Hurricane for quite a while, except for in my mind. We stopped by a few times on our way to or from Grand Marais. Mostly just to savor a wistful look because we had other pressing commitments to attend to, or trout season was past and the river was off-limits to hooks. The last time I was there was during prime autumn glory. Instead of the usual inspiration boost, though, I walked away feeling down. Not really depressed. Just down. Or maybe I wasn't even down. Maybe it was a relative thing. Just the lack of being up or energized, like I expected, made me feel like I was down. Regardless, like most things, the river had changed. A few large trees had fallen across the river atop the falls. Sand had migrated from somewhere, mostly filling the plunge pool. The logjam hole fish hideout, just downstream, was a sand depository, too. It was no longer the river, or at least the stretch of river, in my head.

I knew the river, energized by spring thaws, would likely clean itself up and eventually flush out at least most of the sand. Fish would still migrate upstream. They would just need to find sanctuary somewhere else farther upstream for the time being. Wood comes and goes, just like elsewhere in the forest. Things that I saw as wounds would eventually heal, or maybe change again. In the grand scheme of life and the expanse of time, like many setbacks, this too would prove to be a minor alteration. Still, in the meantime, I'm discussing possibilities with others concerned about the apparent degradation of the stream. Possibilities for a project a short distance upstream at the road crossing that may accelerate healing. In my mind, though, the river will always be the way it was.

I finally returned on a cold but sunny day in mid-May. Julie and I were on our way home from delivering artwork to Grand Marais. She came prepared to paint. I came prepared to fish. Before I pulled out my fishing gear, I took a recon stroll to the waterfall. There was a guy there, landing a steelhead of roughly twenty-four inches. I could see another guy fishing closer to the mouth. That finalized my decision to rig up my 4-weight rod and explore upstream for brook trout, or at least smaller rainbows that had yet to do time out in the lake.

For a hundred yards or so above the H-58 bridge, water was relatively swift, without much in the way of pockets for holding fish. Beyond that, the river held lots of protective wood. So much, in fact, that it not only sheltered any fish that may have been present, it guarded them from fly intrusion and significantly hindered any would-be fly casting. As I explored through the sheltered water, I never actually saw a fish, but I knew there had to be some lurking about somewhere.

After about ninety minutes of "fishing" my way upstream, I came to a two-foot-tall waterfall, spanning the river. It created multiple plunge pools, churning with unknowns. I was sure there were fish in there somewhere, but thirty minutes of fishing with multiple flies resulted in multiple wet flies. Nothing more. Not more than fifty yards upstream from the open mini-falls, overhanging brush and in-stream wood once again dominated the river. At that point, I reeled in my line, hooked my fly to an eyelet, and began bush-whacking back toward the parking area to see how Julie was doing with her painting. My progress was slower than usual because I was being extra cautious about not puncturing or tearing my relatively new neoprene waders. It had taken me three years to finally decide to spend the money on a new pair of waders, and I didn't want to go back to having leaks after only a month of enjoying the dryness. Not catching fish AND screwing up my new waders would be a double whammy that I just didn't want to deal with. I hate having to patch waders during their first season of use, let alone their first month of use.

As I was breaking down my rod at the car, Julie came walking down the road, not having even bothered to finish her painting. From experience, I knew better than to ask to see it. We were apparently in a similar rut. Looking around, I noticed that the guy who had been fishing below the first falls was gone. Not wanting to miss out on an opportunity, I walked over to take a look, even though I didn't expect to see any fish. Apparently, the hole had been vacant of fishermen long enough for fish to resume their activities, because two steelhead were readily visible at the edge of the sandbar. Trying to hurry without drawing attention, I hustled back to the car for my 6-weight rod. Five minutes later I was standing in the shallows below the falls, contemplating a plan. Once again, the guy that was there earlier had been having success using bright orange yarn as imitation spawn. Even though that was a tried-and-true good option for spring, I reasoned that the fish might be wise to that ploy, so I went with a streamer. Something new to get their attention.

Three casts into the plan, I hooked a shiny steelhead that looked to be about twenty inches long. It had been a while since I had something more than an average brook trout on my line. Brook trout are lively when they're on the line, but they lack the raw power of a fresh steelhead. As that raw power made a couple of short surges, I realized that there was no clicking sound as line was being pulled from my reel. Apparently, my drag was set a little too high. Before I could turn the knob to loosen my drag, the fish made a hard run with the current that was churning off the falls. My line went slack as the steelhead pulled loose from the hook. My heart went a little slack, too. To keep from getting too bogged down by the loss, I went back to swinging the streamer. Not many swings later, there was another fish on my line. This one was smaller and duller in color than the first and turned out to be a sucker. It was hooked in the side, so it must have just been an innocent bystander in the wrong place as I was stripping line to pull the streamer back in. I quickly unhooked my accidental catch and let it return to its business. Some people like smoking or pickling suckers. I suppose I could have given it a try if it was a legally hooked fish, but I didn't have any means of keeping a fish cold for the ninety-minute ride home, because I was expecting to be fishing for brook trout, which I rarely keep. Now that I think of it, though, the fact that I brought my 6-weight rod, "just in case," should have triggered thoughts of a cooler. Next time.

Another steelhead was on my line not quite long enough to set the hook, but that was the end of the action. The steelhead had apparently wised up because no matter what I offered in the way of a fly, there was no interest. Often, I could see the fish, but any time my fly came near, it just moved out of the way. It was obvious that I could continue fishing as long as I wanted to, but the catching was over. Julie had already put away her painting supplies and was just taking extra reference pictures while she waited for me. I knew my mom was waiting for us at home, too. Probably not very patiently.

Getting away from the falls, I could hear wind-driven Superior waves working on the nearby beach. It reminded me of the story I had heard about how the Hurricane River acquired its name. Apparently, one of the early European explorers of the region had been pinned down near the mouth of the river during a storm that he had referred to as a hurricane in his notes. I've experienced a few of those storms, but the winds we were experiencing that sunny day certainly didn't conjure up thoughts of a hurricane, and we weren't pinned down due to unsafe lake travel either. So, we got in our car and started the leisurely journey home, leaving the Hurricane and its current residents unbothered for the evening. On the road, I couldn't help thinking about how we've made monumental improvements in transportation and technologies of all kinds, including fishing equipment. But somehow, even with their small brains, fish still have the upper hand.

PANFISH

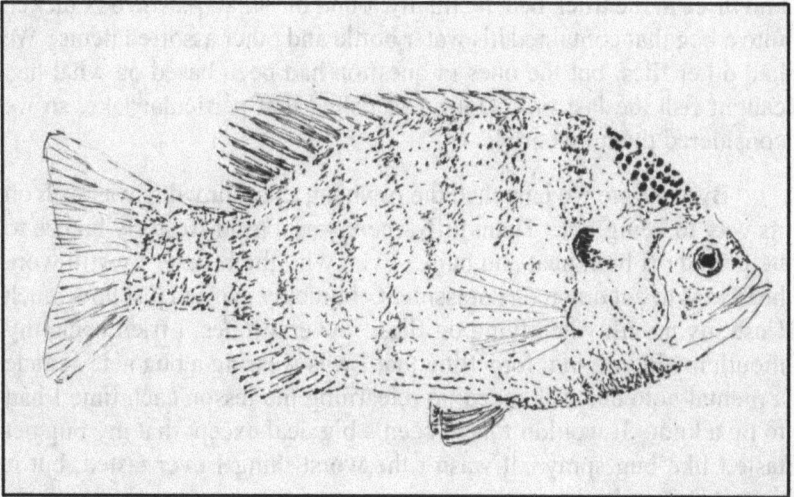

My friend Doug Vanerka and I had been talking about fly fishing for panfish together for a couple of years. Once our schedules aligned and we finally made it past the talking part, we headed out to a small lake in the McCormick Wilderness region. About halfway into our hour-plus drive, I got the sickening feeling that I might not have put my fly rod in the back of Doug's truck when I transferred my gear at his house. It was actually my net that I first thought about. I knew for sure that I didn't grab my net. That got me wondering if I had grabbed my rod. We were too far into the trip to do anything about it. If we had to go back to Doug's house to get my rod, it would screw up our timing for the entire day. Once Doug assured me that he had an extra rod, I was able to let it go and relax. Or I was at least able to not be so tense.

When we reached the small boat launch and began loading our gear into the boat, I was relieved to find that I did have my rod with me, but then it was Doug's turn to panic. He couldn't find the box of flies he had tied specially for the trip. After two looks in the back seat and three in the truck bed, he finally found the small plastic box tucked into a bag that contained his water bottle and other assorted items. We had other flies, but the ones in question had been based on what had caught fish the last time Doug had fished that particular lake, so we considered them essential.

By the time we launched the rowboat, the sunny day was well on its way to being hot. Thankfully, there was a mild westerly breeze to help fend off both heat and bugs. Even with the breeze, we still wore head nets to cut down on harassment. I quickly learned just how much I use my mouth when tying on flies. Several times, I tried using my mouth to aid in tying, forgetting that I was wearing a bug net. I made a mental note but still ended up relearning the lesson each time I had to tie a knot. It wouldn't have been a big deal except that my bug net tasted like bug spray. It wasn't the worst thing I ever tasted, but it certainly wasn't pleasant.

Doug anchored the boat off a rocky point that he knew from past visits. Before I started casting, I just sat in the bow and took a visual tour of the lake. Even with the smattering of cabins, we could have easily been on the edge of the Boundary Waters Canoe Area Wilderness. The rocky shoreline and surrounding north woods forest made me feel at home, even though it was my first time on the lake. It was also my first time fly fishing from a boat. Well, third time, but the first two times were from a canoe, and it felt significantly different. I was sitting in a padded seat with a back on it that was mounted on the metal boat seat. It was a comfortable seat, but it made it difficult for me to turn sideways to cast. Maybe difficult isn't the right description. It was more just awkward. Mentally, it was also a little strange to be casting without having to worry about back cast snags or overhanging branches. I was acutely conscious, though, of the two bodies in the boat that my fly was zinging past with each cast. The fact that we were using weighted streamers added to the concerns floating around in the back of my mind. Every now and then, the sound of the fly passing close by my ear would bring the concern back to the front of my mind.

It took me a bit to get into the proper—meaning successful—cast and retrieve routine. Doug had six or seven fish in the cooler before I landed my first one. At one point, I started mentally preparing myself for the day to be a bust for me. I did have a few temporary hook-ups prior to my first cooler fish, which I gave myself partial credit for. Regardless, it felt good to finally participate in the whole process, not just the casting and retrieval. We were fishing with Mickey Finns and Clouser Minnows. Doug caught one fish on a Mickey Finn and the rest of his initial fish came to a Clouser Minnow. I caught nothing on the Mickey Finn or the Clouser Minnow. Then, just to see what happened, Doug gave me the Clouser Minnow that he was using, which included a streak of green. I tied it on in place of the one that I was using that had a streak of beige. The first cast with the green Clouser brought a fish to the boat. Who would have thought that panfish could be as finicky as trout?

Once I finally started catching fish and settled into more of a proper casting and retrieving routine, my mind began making excursions back in time. One of the places I visited was the canal that bordered the subdivision where I grew up near White Lake. It had a shallow weed bed out in the middle, along with a small brushy island. Besides the small subdivision-owned dock, my friends and I had access to several private docks along the shoreline where we often fished for anything that would take whatever we were fishing with. Our bait typically consisted of nightcrawlers that we caught in our yards by flashlight on wet summer nights. Sometimes, though, we would cast spoons or spinners. Not because we were trying for bigger fish. It just made us feel more grown up to be casting with hardware instead of a nightcrawler and bobber. After a stretch of uneventful casting, we usually switched back to crawlers so we could actually get back to the business of catching fish again. Every now and then, we would haul a boat down to the canal for more serious adventures. Part of the adventure was just getting the boat to the canal. My dad owned an old heavy rowboat that he picked up cheap from a neighbor. Being well under driving age, we used the best means of transportation we had at our disposal— a wheelbarrow. One person would man the wheelbarrow with the back of the boat balanced on it and the other person would walk along, holding up the front of the boat. If the dirt subdivision road was bumpy, balancing the boat on the wheelbarrow could be touchy. The process was difficult enough that we didn't do it often, but sometimes the freedom that came with a boat was just too much to resist.

Another place that bubbled up from my subconscious was a narrow, wooded point of land that stuck out into White Lake. Everyone just referred to it as *The Point*. We never knew who owned it, but we also never got kicked off the property, so nobody worried about it. *The Point* was farther away than the canal, so we didn't fish there quite as often as we did the canal, but the thick woods and slight isolation afforded by *The Point* made it ideal for what felt like real outdoor excursions. For ten- or twelve-year-old kids, it doesn't take much to create memorable adventures. Somehow, those memories don't usually include biting bugs.

By the time Doug and I were ready for lunch, the bugs that kept reminding me of their presence had diminished enough that we could remove our bug nets long enough to eat. Being that I tend to be a prime bug target, and I swell up nicely from the bites, I opted to just roll my net up, so it was above my hat bill. That way, putting it back in place, should the need arise, would only be a matter of seconds. After our lunch break, we moved the boat to where we could cast to nearby shoreline shallows. We had heard fish take something from the surface in that area a few times earlier in the morning. Doug graciously acted as guide and kept the boat in casting position for me while I tossed flies into the shallows. I caught and released a small bass right away, then a small bluegill. After several more unfruitful casts, I finally caught a sizeable enough bluegill to add to the cooler. Following several more uneventful casts, Doug moved the boat to the far side of the rocky point where we had originally started fishing and we continued casting to the shoreline, with occasional lakeward casts. That was where Doug picked up our lone crappie of the day. We were hoping for more, as they typically hang out in small schools, but the bonanza never materialized. We did catch a couple more small bass as well as two more sub-cooler 'gills, but the frequency was certainly diminishing.

During the mix of afternoon fishing and reminiscing, the breeze went from relaxingly refreshing to a minor casting opponent. That allowed me to create a couple of breeze-induced wind knots that gave me a casting break while I put on my reading glasses to untangle the mess. One knot was good enough to require a tippet start-over. After several fruitless minutes, I finally had to cut my tippet and my pride and admit defeat.

I had an evening commitment, so our fishing time was limited. As our necessary departure time drew near, the clear blue afternoon sky took on a haziness with scattered but unobtrusive clouds. That was about when the mild breeze crossed the line to a steady breeze with minor gusts. It probably wasn't an issue for Doug, but for me, it became a little more challenging. It was a good time to trailer the boat and begin the trek home.

Bugs greeted us at the boat launch, but in the heat of the day, it wasn't the fanfare we received earlier in the morning. On the way home, as with most fishing outings, we talked about when we would come back. When the 'gills were more consistently in shallow water where they would hit topwater flies was our conclusion. No date was set, but a commitment was made. I think all fishing trips have to include a discussion about *next time*. It's not a written rule. It's just something we can't help doing. Even in the event that a fishing trip is a complete bust, there is almost always a plan for a return trip to redeem yourself. I think the success of an outing can often be based on how early in the trip someone brings up the idea of a return visit. In this case, it was while we were still fishing. I believe it was shortly after lunch. As we talked about a return trip again on our way home, it dawned on me that this was the first time that I brought home some fish to eat in a long time.

When I was a kid, bringing home fish was a common occurrence. Of course, in those days, our biggest concern was coming home empty-handed, so any fish was an eater. The fact that we didn't have a self-imposed panfish size limit made bringing home fish easy. These days, my usual outings are catch and release ventures for brook trout, so a successful day means coming home with fish adventures in my head and nothing in the cooler. In fact, I don't even bring a cooler. Having a cooler with fish in it again, though, got me thinking about how I wanted to cook them.

Of course, before I could cook and eat them, I had to clean them. That, too, had been a long time since I last did it. I had never done much filleting. When I was a kid, most of the panfish we caught were too small to fillet, so we just scaled them and removed the head and fins. As I got older, other things began vying for my time, and pursuing panfish simply faded away except for a few times with my daughters. After Doug and I enjoyed our successful day on that quiet lake in the forest, I found myself regretting letting panfish slip from my radar. I especially regretted not more earnestly reviving the pursuit as my kids were growing up. At one point in my panfish ponderings, I even began thinking that maybe I owed my daughters an apology. As I was scaling and cleaning the twenty-three fish we brought home that day, I decided that a formal apology might be overreacting just a little. Maybe just spending some time chasing panfish with my granddaughters would make me feel better. I made a mental note to find out.

In the meantime, I simply cooked some of the fish on our charcoal grill and carefully peeled the meat from the bones. They tasted even better than I remembered.

THE PORKIES

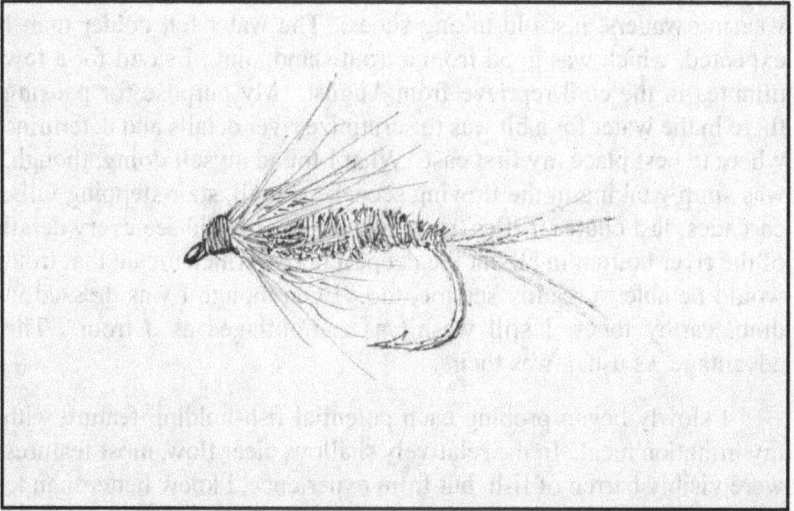

I was working on exploring the Porcupine Mountains Wilderness State Park (more commonly known as *The Porkies*) through its waterways. For the smaller streams, a fly rod seemed to be the logical explorational tool. So, there I stood on the wooden footbridge, rod in hand, watching the Little Union trickle past. Water volume was considerably less than I expected, even for August. It certainly didn't look like trout water. Then again, I had seen some sizeable fish come out of streams that a kindergartener could've readily hopped across without making a splash. Still, I was concerned about stressing the fish too much in such small water during the August heat, so I decided to retrace my steps back down the trail to the Union River.

The Union wasn't carrying what I would call an abundance of water either, but it at least looked more like a river than a chub creek. Besides, I had been wanting to fish that stretch of water since first

111

seeing it several months earlier. When I was a hundred yards or so past the confluence with the Little Union, I strung up my fly rod, tied on a general attractor pattern, and stepped in.

With warm weather and relatively shallow water, I wasn't wearing waders, just old hiking shoes. The water felt colder than I expected, which was good from a trout standpoint. I stood for a few minutes in the cool reprieve from August. My purpose for pausing there in the water for a bit was to scrutinize river details and determine where to best place my first cast. What I found myself doing, though, was simply taking in the flowing scenery. Small, stair-stepping falls, cascades, fast chutes, riffles, runs, and pools. I could see every detail of the river bottom in all but the deepest pools, which meant that trout would be able to readily see me, too. Even though I was dressed in drab, earthy tones, I still wasn't as camouflaged as a trout. The advantage, as usual, was theirs.

I slowly began probing each potential fish-holding feature with my imitation meal. In the relatively shallow, clear flow, most features were visibly barren of fish, but from experience, I knew better than to simply trust my vision. So I continued probing each feature as I slowly ventured upstream. For the most part, I wouldn't say that I was actually casting. Due to close quarters and well-placed vegetation, more often than not what guided my fly was more of a flick or a wave of the rod tip. Whatever was needed to place the fly where it needed to be or, in some cases, close to where it needed to be.

One particular spot was not visibly barren of fish. The trout in question looked to be a rainbow of about ten inches. It was tucked under the curvature of an enormous boulder in a location that was plainly visible yet maddeningly difficult to get a fly into. The spot that I envisioned I needed to be was easily visible to the fish and already occupied by a sprawling tree branch. I stepped back and watched from a distance, trying to develop a plan. The plan I finally settled on was to quietly continue my tour upstream.

That's where I found an old stone and cement foundation section that looked like a short wall extending across the river. Near the middle, there was a broken-out section a few feet wide, creating a fast chute that emptied into a dark hole in the sandstone riverbed.

112

Several times my fly swirled through the pool, sometimes visible, sometimes not. With each pass, my hope faded. Then came the flashing of a fish and the pulsing of my line. The small rainbow thrashed its way up from the darkness and into my net. It wasn't the colorfully painted brook trout that I was hoping for, but it was a trout, and a wild one at that. A steelhead smolt, most likely, waiting for the proper time in its lifecycle to move out to the Big Lake, where it would grow and mature until it was ready to return to the river to start another generation of fish. As I turned the shiny-sided trout loose from the confines of my net, it bolted back to its secret hideout in the darkness without the slightest hesitation.

I lingered for a time, thinking about that fish and how dependent it was not only on the river but the entire Union River watershed. Actually, the entire Lake Superior watershed would affect that fish during the course of its life, much like all of us who live, or even recreate, here near the Big Lake.

Those thoughts continued to swirl through my head as I slowly worked my way up the river, past the old iron bridge, and on up through the slight canyon, to where the Union passes beneath South Boundary Road.

I saw a few other small trout, but none came to my net. One did rise up from the safety of a rock-undercut fortress to dance with my fly for a moment as it spun in the swirling current. The fish, caught up in the same swirl, stared at my fly, working on its decision, as they both slowly rotated in a clockwise circle. The fish ultimately decided that something wasn't right and casually descended back down to the safety of its hiding place beneath the undercut.

Fishing up through the canyon proved to be difficult. Not because of difficult flow characteristics or slipperiness of the rocks but because of scenic distractions. Stair-step cascades over moss-covered rock, lichen-accented walls rising up into the forest from the river, and shade-producing trees contributing an air of lushness. Being there was worthwhile, regardless of fish in the net or not. Fishing became intermingled with sightseeing, or maybe sightseeing became intermingled with fishing. It was difficult to tell which was the dominant activity.

The twin convoluted steel culverts—both probably ten feet in diameter—carrying the Union flow under South Boundary Road marked the end of my outing, not because of lack of fish or fishable water beyond but because my time for the day's adventure was winding down. A collection of logs and sticks against the upstream end of the culverts throttled down the flow, leaving water in the structures only a few inches deep. Looking up through one of the tunnels, the kid in me just couldn't resist, so I carefully waded on through and climbed out over the barricade of wooden debris.

I considered continuing on for a bit, regardless of the time. Then I realized that I had already accomplished what I had set out to do. I had fished the river that I so often envisioned fishing during our January stay in the park—dancing with trout and even admiring one in my hand. I had stepped into the refreshing flow, felt its pulse, and been part of its existence. After spending some time rejuvenating in our natural world, I was leaving it unscathed for anyone who would come after me. Continuing on would have been fun, I'm sure, but it was time to go. Time to have a bite to eat and to reflect in the flicker of a campfire flame. It was time to go sit beside the expanse of Superior, look out to the fading horizon, and begin dreaming of tomorrows.

During one of those tomorrows, sunlight mingled with a misty haze through the hemlocks as my wife and I stood on the bridge near Overlooked Falls, surveying the Little Carp River. The air felt heavy with moisture. Not quite to the point of a sauna but more like a closed-up bathroom after a hot shower. I could see it in the hazy shafts of light that penetrated the shadowed forest. Just looking at the river felt like a refreshing drink. I was tempted to rig up my fly rod and step into the sparkling flow right there at the bridge, but I didn't really know the river, so I knew it would be more fruitful to do a little more exploring and watching from the trail first. Even without the heat and humidity, my first temptation is always to just step right in as soon as I arrive at a river before I even attempt to look things over and size up the situation. Besides, I wanted to fish my way up the river, not down. So, I held back my temptation to plunge in, and we headed off down the trail to see what promising-looking water we could find.

Our pace was quicker than normal for studying the water because I wanted to cover some ground before I committed to fishing for fear that there might be a better-looking spot just a little farther downstream.

As we passed the cabin near Greenstone Falls, I found myself feeling a little envious of the family that was staying there. Besides having a gorgeous view, they were perched right in the middle of an enticing stretch of trout water, with the sounds of the river permeating the forest.

A little north of Greenstone Falls Cabin, the trail climbed a ridge to skirt around a small camp area. Up on the ridge, the river was far enough away that details were not really discernible. We could see the river but not well enough to evaluate fishing possibilities. After what seemed like at least half a mile, the trail finally dropped back down from the ridge and onto a flat floodplain. We took the opportunity to wander back over near the river.

I was tempted to continue following the river, but I did want to actually fish, not just survey the possibilities. I probably should've just rigged up there and started fishing, but I really liked the looks of the water farther upstream, from the camp area on up to the bridge near Overlooked Falls. That stretch was likely fished pretty heavily and had more foot traffic right along the riverbank, but I still decided that was where I wanted to fish, so we headed back upstream along the trail. By then, I wasn't really taking in the scenery as much as just covering ground so that I could start fishing.

Standing on the bedrock formations a short way below Greenstone Falls, I found it difficult to get my fly rod rigged up because I kept staring at the river instead of my gear. When I finally stepped into the flow, the chill of the water was like opening a refrigerator on a hot, sultry day. As with the previous day's fishing, I was wading wet to avoid having to haul my waders around. Most of the water was relatively shallow anyway, making waders, or even hip boots, hot and cumbersome. So I was wading wet, which is a refreshing way to go in August when you're fishing relatively shallow streams with a good solid bottom. I pointed my wet shoes upstream and began fishing.

Just below the falls, I was floating my fly over a small hole that was guarded by a sizeable boulder. I watched a nine-inch brook trout rise up from the shadows and quickly snatch my fly. The frenzied pulsing at the end of my line was as refreshing as the flow. After taking the fish from my net and briefly admiring its wild flare, I opened my hand and watched it dart back to the unknown.

Not far above the falls, I was fishing my way through a swift run when I was surprised to catch a glimpse of a trout that looked to be about twelve inches long shoot out in front of me and race downstream. It had been holding near a log in the shallows by the riverbank. My attention had been focused on the run that was closer to the middle of the river. Before I spooked the fish, I did take a look around, but I blew off the shallow water near the bank in favor of the run, which I thought was a much better bet. As it turned out, I lost that bet.

I saw a few other trout that afternoon, but none came to my net. I did get the satisfaction, though, of fishing water I had been wanting to fish for several months. I had finally lived the adventure I had been picturing in my mind, just without as many fish. Due to easy access and proximity to a couple of popular waterfalls, I knew the stretch I had chosen to fish was probably well-used, not only by people fishing but by general sightseers as well. It could also have been the mostly sunny, muggy day, or maybe my choice of fly patterns. My presentation of the fly may not have been at its best either. It's usually easy to come up with a list of reasons for a day short on fish. Still, exploring with my fly rod, I had the privilege of being an active participant in the life of the river. Even though I was traveling in the opposite direction as the river, I was flowing over the rocks just the same.

Not long before I reached the bridge where I had planned to end my explorations, I came across a young boy that I guessed was probably about seven or eight years old. He was playing in the middle of the river, moving rocks and splashing around as kids often do, while a lady that I presumed was his mother lounged on the far bank and watched. I was a bit bummed that I had to get out of the water in order to politely go around him without intruding on his space. I wasn't upset, or even irritated, really, just a little bothered about the interruption. Still, I was pleasant about it, smiling at the boy and nodding to the mother. After all, they weren't doing anything wrong.

As I was stepping back into the river, just upstream, it occurred to me that when I was his age, I would no doubt have been playing in the water, too. Then the thought hit me that I *am* playing in the water. In fact, I've been playing in the water most of my life. It may not keep me physically young, but I do believe it's at least part of what keeps me young at heart and always planning new adventures.

I looked back at the boy again and gave him a nod of approval. He didn't see me, but I felt I needed to do it anyway. Hopefully, he'll never lose that youthful urge to play in the water.

There wasn't much river left to fish before my planned exit point. It was mostly just the plunge pools below a couple of small falls. With the pools being much deeper than anywhere else I had fished that day, I'm sure I didn't have enough weights on the line to get my fly down to where it needed to be to entice a fish. At that point, it didn't really matter anyway. Sometimes, just the act of fishing and the anticipation that comes with it are all it takes to satisfy my need for adventure. For me, just stepping into the flow often provides the connection I need.

Later, as I stood dripping on the bridge above Overlooked Falls, my young friend walked by with his parents. I wanted to say something to them, but I couldn't think of anything that I thought would sound appropriate. So, I simply smiled and nodded. We had all simply enjoyed the river for a time. There was no need to discuss details.

The following May, I was back in the park to fish the Little Iron River in the Nonesuch Falls area. A welcoming party of mosquitoes greeted me at the trailhead as I was getting my gear ready to go. On a day when temperatures were predicted to get into the eighties, I would normally opt to wade wet. But, as I was liberally dowsing myself with bug spray, I decided that some extra protection would be a good idea, so I pulled on my waders in between swats. The belt that I always wear to keep most of the river on the outside, should I lose my footing, doubled as a good bug barrier to keep the biters on the outside, too.

It was only about 8:00 a.m., but the thermometer was rising fast. I expected the hike to the river would be hot and buggy but was pleasantly surprised to find that I was wrong. There was just enough shade to moderate the heat, and the bugs apparently decided to wait at the trailhead for the next potential meal instead of following me. I had no idea why—they usually just swarm the first candidate and keep at it—but I considered it one of those blessings that I don't understand and just said, "Thank you."

With my mind set on fishing, I only gave the Nonesuch mine site ruins a few passing glances on my way through to the river. Like most ghost towns, it seemed to have a lonely air about it, like it was waiting for its wayward souls to return.

When I emerged from the riverside trees, I was surprised by how shallow the river was. With the calendar page still on May, I expected the flow to be much more substantial. I guess it shouldn't have been such a surprise because we had experienced moderate snow during the winter and a relatively slow spring melt that started early. Spring rains had been frugal as well, leaving most of the streams near home— which was only a few hours away—looking like late August. The Little Iron River proved to be no different.

The plunge pool at the base of Nonesuch Falls looked like my best fishing prospect, so after looking it over for a few minutes, I rigged up my fly rod and began plying its depths with a bead-headed nymph. After fifteen minutes of wetting the nymph, I switched over to a yellow stimulator because I refused to believe that there wasn't a trout in the pool. First, I tried dropping the fly directly into the falls and letting it tumble into the pool. Then, I tried dropping it here, there, and anywhere I hadn't yet tried.

Although water cascaded into the pool across most of the width of the river, there was more of a concentrated flow coming into the south side, so I focused more of my attention on that area. Overall, though, I pretty well covered the entire pool from a variety of casting locations.

After another fifteen minutes or so of imagining each cast was going to be the one, I still wasn't convinced that the pool held nothing but water. My intention for the day, though, wasn't strictly fishing. I wanted to explore a decent stretch of the Little Iron just for the sake of seeing the sights and getting to know the river. With that in mind,

I bid the pool—and probably a few fish—goodbye and began slowly working my way upstream, tossing a fly any place that looked like it might hold a fish.

The entire river bottom was solid bedrock strewn with small collections of rock fragments and slabs. Woody cover was sparse. In fact, calling it sparse is being generous. Still, it was a beautiful little river with its interesting bottom contours and formations, riffles and runs, cascades, chutes, and bends. Due to low water levels, though, most of the holes were not really holes. They were more like smooth depressions, extending the water depth to twelve inches instead of six. Even with the reddish iron tint of the water, bottom features were clearly visible most everywhere. Fish were not.

I continued my upstream exploration for roughly three hours without hooking—or even seeing—a fish. Well, that's not quite true. I did see a few minnows, but instead of seeing a few minnows at a time, as is usually the case, I only saw a few minnows. Period.

Besides the lack of cover, I later suspected that the water temperature may have been getting a little too warm as well. Especially for that early in the year. Unfortunately, the idea of getting out my thermometer and checking didn't occur to me until later in the evening when I was reflecting on the day's events while gazing into a campfire. So, I couldn't really say if the water temperature was an issue or not. You would think that I would have thought of something important like that while I was still on the river, but, being so early in the season, water temperatures getting too high isn't a typical issue, so it just didn't click.

As the heat and bugs both continued to increase, I decided to turn around and do some exploring below the falls. At that point, I considered fishing the falls pool again but decided to explore some more new water instead. I was torn between focusing on the best potential fish-holding water at hand or simply exploring a new area of the park. With heat and bugs beginning to make fishing difficult, I opted to continue downstream to just see the sights, test some new water, and see if I could find another good-looking fishing spot.

Just like above the falls, there wasn't much in the way of cover in the water. I found a lot of beautiful water flowing over interesting, sculpted rock but no fish. I explored down to where the old road or railroad grade crossed the river, then a little beyond that. I was finally beginning to find some woody cover in the river. In fact, there was a sizeable logjam where I made my final casts. As I was closely watching my fly, taking great care not to do anything to disturb its natural drift, I was also watching mosquitoes lining up along the knuckles of my rod hand. Anything I did to shoo them away also resulted in an unnatural behavior of my fly. As I contemplated a remedy, beads of sweat were beginning to ooze out from under my hatband and trickle down my forehead.

At that point, I decided that the best remedy would be to move my explorations to somewhere with at least a mild breeze to keep bugs and heat at bay. So, at least on that particular day, the trout around Nonesuch Falls turned out to be none.

My roughly three-quarter-mile, wader-clad stroll back out to the trailhead was relatively bug-free. As long as I was moving, biting bugs seemed to be absent. I assumed that maybe the heat had them feeling a bit lethargic, so they didn't bother to chase me. Normally the mid-eighty-degree heat would have me feeling lethargic, too, but it somehow didn't seem to bother me much. Maybe I was just so appreciative of the lack of blackflies and mosquitoes that other annoyances went unnoticed.

As for the fishing, I had experienced some similar rivers in the Upper Peninsula before. High on visual aesthetics. Low on fish. Persistence usually pays off in those cases. In this case, the heat and bugs had simply out-persisted my persistence. Still, I found that even a day of fishing that ended up just being a day of exploring new water while wetting some flies was a worthwhile endeavor, as it usually is. Fortunately, I wasn't counting on having fish for dinner. Hopefully, my wife, Julie, wasn't either.

NATIVE

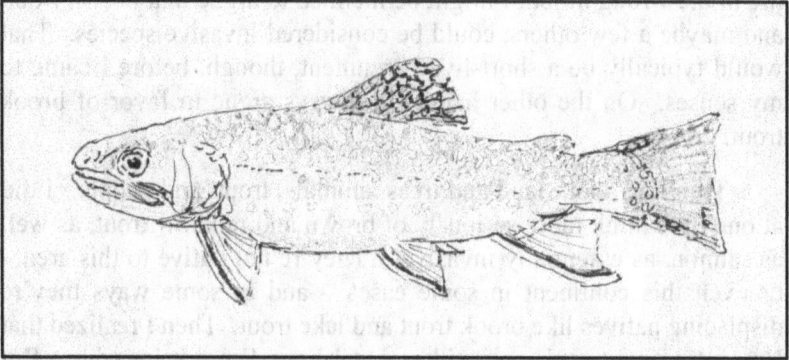

I have a thing for wild brook trout. Speckled trout, as I understand old-timers called them. For one thing, they're incredibly beautiful, especially in their autumn spawning attire. For another thing, where I live, they're native. They belong here. They're a long-standing part of the local environment, like the bedrock and cobble that north woods streams flow through. And they're the essence of wild. All wild animals and fish are technically wild, but trout, especially native trout, seem to me to be the epitome of wildness. Before I go getting all mushy, let's just go back to my original statement. I have a thing for brook trout. Especially wild brook trout in wild water. No explanation or apology. I just do.

Maybe my love of and fascination for brook trout is at least partly because I, too, am native to Michigan. I was born and raised in Michigan, have lived here all my life, and I fully expect to die here – or at least be buried here if I happen to die while on a trip somewhere. Brook trout are one of the few trout and salmonoids that can claim Michigan as native waters. For me, things that are native to an area are special and important to that area. I love to fish for and catch brook

121

trout, but I also love to protect them and the environment that they need to survive. I will always stand up for and defend brook trout. I don't like to kill them, even though I know they taste great. Even though I have a fondness for all trout and salmon, if you were to catch me in the wrong mood, I might be inclined to argue that brown trout, and maybe a few others, could be considered invasive species. That would typically be a short-lived argument, though, before I came to my senses. On the other hand, I'll always argue in favor of brook trout.

Thinking about land and trees, animals, trout, and people. I did at one time think more seriously of brown and rainbow trout, as well as salmon, as essentially invasives. They're not native to this area – or even this continent in some cases – and in some ways they're displacing natives like brook trout and lake trout. Then I realized that I'm not native to this area either, but I hope I'm not invasive. I'm trying hard to enhance and protect our surroundings, not degrade them or change them for the worse. I'm certainly not trying to displace anyone either. If we go back enough generations, none of us are native to this area or any area in America. Unless the Garden of Eden was here in the Upper Peninsula, literally none of us have family trees that originated here. Same goes for most anyplace else. We all immigrated, migrated, or were brought to where we are now at some point in our lineage. From that standpoint, even the Indian nations are non-native if you go back in time far enough. So, maybe the question or issue isn't so much native vs. non-native, it's beneficial vs. destructive, or maybe enhancing vs. degrading. The goal, of course, is to be beneficial and enhancing, making things better because we're here.

Now that you're either nodding your head in agreement, or shaking your fists in disagreement, the questions that need to be raised are, What exactly constitutes classification as native, and why does it matter? Or does it matter?

I grew up downstate. The lower part of the Lower Peninsula. For many years, up north was a far-away place.

Up north. I would get dreamy-eyed any time I heard those words. It's been like that ever since I was a young kid. Up north meant summer vacations in most cases. Camping and campfires, sightseeing, historic sites, trails, lakes, rivers, collecting cool things that I found (mostly rocks). Up north meant the smell of woodsmoke and pine. Sandy earth and water. It meant freedom to roam and explore. Up north, of course, is a relative term, but it described someplace that meant the world to me. I couldn't get enough.

As I got a little older, there were hunting and fishing trips with my dad. Sometimes it was just the two of us. Other times, usually for fishing, some of Dad's friends were involved, too. Salmon and steelhead fishing on the Platte River spawned some of my fondest outdoor memories. My dad's friend Bob Johnson would bring his son Bobby, who was about my age. While our dads fished, we had the run of the countryside. As long as we stayed together and let our dads know where we were going, we were free to roam. And roam we did. Up and down the Platte, exploring fallen trees and logjams, peering at hiding fish through dark windows between tree roots in the riverbank, following small tributaries, rock hunting in an old gravel pit. We were everywhere our dreams and imaginations would take us. Every now and then, we would check in to show we were still alive, then back out on another adventure. We couldn't have been more than ten or eleven years old at the time, because I think I started participating in the fishing about the time I turned twelve. Grand adventures that set the stage for a lifetime of up north yearnings.

Once I got into actually fishing for salmon and steelhead, new dreams and adventures arose. Up before daylight, waiting on the bank for sunrise near our favorite hole to make sure we got there first. Probing the depths of holes and logjams for those tantalizing ghostly forms that waved in the blurry current. The Colorado spinner on the end of my monofilament line was part of me, or I was part of it. When we would hook into a fish, the eight-and-a-half-foot fly rod would nearly double over in response to the pure wildness on the end of my line. The exhilaration was intoxicating. It was up north.

A little later in life, when it came time to pick a college, where else could I go but up north? Way up north. Houghton. Michigan Tech. My passions expanded to include trout fishing, rock climbing, ice climbing, snowshoeing, and cross-country skiing. The short visits of my youth now stretched into nine-month ventures. Dad passed away near the end of my sophomore year at Tech. Maybe I should have transferred to somewhere closer to home after that, but the thought never crossed my mind. Going back up north the following fall was the only option that I saw.

Early years of work and marriage, though based downstate, were filled with trips north at every opportunity. It was where I wanted to be. I was drawn north again and again. Graduate school, back at Michigan Tech, quenched the up north thirst for a couple of years, but then it was back downstate for work and venturing north whenever possible. After our daughters, Amy and Megan, entered our lives, up north shriveled to a once-or-twice-a-year vacation. At the time, it was fine, because we had a different focus as young parents and family providers. Over time, though, the old call got louder again. Our response was to buy land and build a log cabin. Up north of course. Near Paradise – where else? The project took most of a year. Actually, it's not truly finished yet, nearly thirty years later. But we have been enjoying time there all along anyway.

Since building our cabin connection to the north woods, up north expanded to include Isle Royale and northeastern Minnesota, but it still mostly meant northern Michigan. In my mind, the southern limit was always Clare, because that's where you hit that invisible line where everything suddenly looks, feels, and smells like the north woods. Amy eventually went up north for college at Northern Michigan University, in Marquette. Megan soon followed suit by enrolling at Lake Superior State University, in Sault Saint Marie. During those college years, our trips north increased in frequency and became more regular events. That's when the bug to move north started digging its pinchers into me and Julie. It just felt *right* whenever we were up north. The cabin, Marquette, the Soo, Superior's north shore, Boundary Waters Canoe Area Wilderness. It didn't matter. We felt at home, like we belonged there, even though we were still just visitors. I remember sitting on the deck, savoring fresh Lake Superior fish at *The Angry Trout* in Grand Marais, Minnesota, when Julie and I both said, "I could live here." We didn't necessarily mean right there in Grand Marais but up north, somewhere.

That yearning burned for several years, through numerous trips and dreams. "I could live here," echoed in my head. That thought eventually grew into, I want to live there. I dreamed. I schemed. We visited. Amy graduated from college and she and her husband, Kyle, decided to stay near Marquette. The desire burned hotter. Emptiness in my stomach when we headed south after a visit deepened. I yearned to be up north and looked for any excuse for a visit. Then one afternoon, my job of twenty-five years, the primary anchor holding us downstate, was suddenly gone. At first, I was devastated. Then, after several weeks, I began looking at the blank slate of life in front of us, and the fact that both our daughters now lived in the Upper Peninsula. If we had to start over anyway, why not move the restart north?

We took a UP reconnaissance trip in May, just to check out the housing situation. Julie wanted to look everywhere. I was moving to the Keweenaw. After a week of unsuccessful searching, which was prefaced with a few months of internet searches, we found nothing that fit our wants or needs. As we were preparing to retreat back downstate, with me feeling utterly dejected, Julie suggested that we check with the realtor she had talked to on our way through Munising. I didn't want to move to the Munising area, but our other options weren't looking so good. With a tight feeling in my gut, I understandingly responded, "Whatever!"

The place that Patty found for us to look at was in Deerton. The house wasn't what we ideally wanted, but it came with one hundred and sixty acres of land. "Okay, we'll look." The house wasn't as rustic-looking as I had hoped, but we could work with it. The property was more to my liking. Two more visits the next day and it was looking better each time. It was less than an hour away from our kids. The same for the Pictured Rocks National Lakeshore. Trout streams, wilderness areas, and National Forest lands were all around. Were we serious about moving or not? We decided to pull the trigger, made an offer, and headed for home. As soon as the offer was accepted, we put our farm up for sale and went public with our plans, which were received with mixed reactions. Four and a half sweaty, hard-working months later, the farm was sold. Thanksgiving weekend, we loaded up multiple personal vehicles and a twenty-six-foot rental truck and headed north.

Having lived on that historic farm for twenty years and raising our kids there, I expected our departure to be relatively traumatic. For me, though, the transition time was about thirty seconds—as I was pulling out of the farm driveway and heading off down Behling Road. Once we hit the road, the past twenty years, fun and adventurous as they were, were in the rearview mirror. In the windshield was up north. It had been a long road that took years to traverse, but the Deerton place felt like home the very first night. Destinations that at one time were hours away are now within minutes. Lake Superior is now in our neighborhood. We see it all the time and visit whenever we want. The north woods is our yard. We've been accepted into the Yooper family. Up north, once the distant land of dreams, is now our everyday reality. It's home.

About five months after we moved here, it dawned on me while I was lying in bed, that we're here. We are here to stay, God willing. Why it took me so long for that fact to sink in, I don't know. Maybe I was just too preoccupied with moving and moving in. My body and mind were finally settling into being home in this place. We were meeting people, making connections, making friends, making commitments, getting involved, looking to belong and be part of this place, not just visitors. Even at our cabin, some three hours away, we're now locals, not just people from downstate who happen to venture up now and then to borrow the feel of the north woods. We live in the north woods. We are now part of the north woods, although I think in my heart I always have been. I love visiting out west and the northeast portions of the country, but I've never really imagined myself living there. I've always been fine with visiting. Not so with up north. Living up north has long been a dream. I sort of lived up north a bit when I was in college at Michigan Tech, but then it was still only temporary. A long visit but a visit just the same. I didn't set down roots. I enjoyed the Keweenaw, but it was still temporary, and I knew it. So did everyone else. We were expected to leave eventually. Not so now. We expect to stay. People expect us to stay. We're members at church, not guests. We're taking part in the community, not just passing through, maybe spending a few dollars, and moving on. It's more than just vacationland. It's home. We're locals. We're getting to know the people at the bank, post office, and stores. We met the garbage man. We have a normal place to shop. We're developing routines, wrapping our arms around our property, and getting to know its details. This area has become our area. This has become our place. We care about it. We want to help other people who live here. We're home. Sure, we'll still travel some. We'll probably go out west now and then. We'll still spend time relaxing along Superior's north shore and haunt the Boundary Waters Canoe Area Wilderness, maybe even more so now that we live closer. The difference will be that as Yoopers, we'll be locals around the lake. We'll have a connection with those places and the people that live there. We're neighbors. North woods residents. I'm like a wild steelhead. I didn't originate here, but I have naturalized, found my niche, and become part of the wild landscape. I may not technically be native to this place, but I'm wild and free and I hope I'm enhancing the natural community by being here.

In *The Strangest Secret*, the late author and motivator Earl Nightengale said that you become what you think about. Well, I have thought about the north woods and waters for many years. Through time and blessings, I am now sure enough part of the north woods and waters. We didn't move here because land was cheaper or to get away from certain things, although the crowded craziness of many other places is good to get away from. Our move north was a conscious decision to follow through on a dream and an opportunity that I believe God provided. We didn't come here to change the north country. We changed, at least in some ways, to become part of the north country. This may very well have been part of God's grand plan for me all along. Maybe I just needed some other training and experience before I was ready. A lot of other training, in fact. Fifty-four years' worth to be exact. Or maybe it just took me a while to catch on and recognize the grand plan. Anyway, we're here now, an inseparable part of the north country. We may not be natives by history, but we're certainly natives by heart. Hopefully, that counts for something.

I once saw a home décor sign at a friend's house that stated, *All that we love deeply becomes part of us*. I believe it goes further than that. I think that we often also become part of it as well. In a way, we naturalize and become an integral part of our surroundings, hopefully without ousting or offsetting anything or anyone that was already here.

Getting back to my original thought, I have a thing for wild brook trout. And I certainly hope they are around for generations of people well beyond my lifetime to have a thing for them too. Whether I'm considered native or not, I'm doing my best to help that happen.

SUPERIOR NORTH SHORE

I had been eyeing Superior north shore streams for years, but our shoreline stays were always for only a day or two, and usually involved the whole family. I didn't feel right about taking considerable time – and money – just for me to fish. Then, my wife Julie started participating in the Plein Air Grand Marais painting competition. That expanded our Superior north shore time to more than a week, providing me time to indulge myself. With the opportunity to fish for more than just a few hours, the $53 non-resident license wasn't as painful either.

The first year Julie participated in the painting event, streams were running alarmingly low, and as a result, warm. I knew that I really shouldn't be applying even more pressure to the fish by trying to catch them. In those conditions, even catch-and-release can, and often is fatal. But I had brought my fishing stuff with me and had been

129

planning to fish some north shore streams for several months. Hoping to find someone to assure me that things were not as bad as I thought, I stopped by a local fly shop to get the inside scoop. The owner and guide reluctantly confirmed my concerns, which I could appreciate was difficult. After all, if I was able to go fishing, he would have at least been able to sell me a handful of flies and maybe even have a shot at doing some guiding. I, in turn, appreciated the fact that he was concerned enough about the welfare of the local stream ecology to turn away a potential income for the good of the fish. I went ahead and bought a couple of small things, just because it felt like the right thing to do. Then I turned my attention to pursuing agates instead of trout, which was a similar endeavor in that it involved finding mostly a bunch of small ones. The one big one that I found wasn't an agate. It was a relatively large ribbon rock, much like the boulder I've seen pictures of that resides on the Isle of Pines, within the Boundary Waters Canoe Area Wilderness. The rock I found was big enough to require a tractor to haul it, so it's still where I found it, unless subsequent raging spring flows have moved it to a new hiding spot.

The following year, September conditions in northern Minnesota were much better, so I bought the handful of flies and sprung for a non-resident license. On the first day of fishing, I left Julie painting a shoreline scene near the Cascades River mouth and began working my way upstream. Anticipating the possibility of steelhead or salmon in the lower reaches, I opted for a 6-weight rod instead of my usual trout fishing 4-weight. That worked out fine because, along Minnesota's Superior shoreline, pretty much every stream entering the Big Lake has special coaster brook trout regulations in an effort to help our region's iconic fish make a comeback. Because of that, I was not supposed to be fishing for brook trout below the first major falls anyway, regardless of their size.

My first cast was just above the Highway 61 bridge. Even though the habitat looked good, I couldn't seem to find any fish in the neighborhood. Before I continued upstream, three guys with spinning gear started working on the hole beneath the bridge. I hung around for a bit, going through the motions of fishing just to see what they were able to accomplish without looking like I was watching them. Fifteen minutes later, they were still at zero fish, too. I felt a little better as I moved on. Apparently, it wasn't just me.

I worked my way to the tail of the big exotic blue-green pool right below the first tall falls. I had seen others fishing there during previous visits and had felt a bit envious as I spectated from the trail above. As I scrutinized the clear water from my riverside rocky perch, I didn't see any fish, but there were ample nooks and crannies for fish to hide in addition to the deeper, darker areas of the hole. It looked like a good opportunity to wet some streamers. For more than thirty minutes, streamer wetting went well. I began getting the impression, though, that there may not have been any fish present in the pool to care. After several more casts, just because I finally could, I reeled in and hooked up my fly. Looking up, I noticed a guy up top near the trail, leaning on the wooden safety fence. Even though I couldn't make out his facial features or expression, I understood his desire to be living in the scene. It felt good being the person down in the ravine at water level, casting a fly, fish or no fish. Being a trout fishing participant is always much more satisfying than being a spectator.

The only way out was to backtrack most of the way to the bridge, so I decided that I might as well check in on Julie's painting progress before exploring farther upstream. She was having more success than me, so I swapped rods for my favorite 4-weight and took the trail to the top of the falls gorge. The water was considerably lower and skinnier than below the falls, but it still seemed fishable. I soon came to realize that there was not an abundance of fish-holding pockets. Not far above the uppermost falls, though, I did manage to hook a fish in a slight foam line along a vertical rock face. The energetic trout looked to be about nine inches long, but it shook free of the hook shortly after our initial connection, so I never got the opportunity to verify my estimate. Just upstream, a long dark hole produced another fish of similar size. It studied my fly twice and twice backed down into the dark. After that, it was apparently disinterested, or maybe just enough smarter to know better.

I continued on for another couple hundred yards without encountering any other fish. There were most likely some fish there to encounter. I either didn't present the right fly, or I presented the right fly in the wrong way. Regardless, I didn't find any more trout. I did finally have an active day on a north shore river, though, and I did find some trout. Satisfied with my progress, I meandered back down to the river mouth to hook up with Julie. While she finished the last bit of her painting, I roamed the rocky shoreline, looking for whatever caught my eye. What I found, at the end of the longest point of rock in the vicinity was the shape of a jumping trout protruding from the bedrock. It looked like it had been created by chipping away the surrounding rock to leave the raised side view of an arched fish. There were no visible tool marks, so I assumed it had been there for some time, with the occasional lapping of waves keeping it moist. I found it ironic that I had spent a good share of the day searching for that very creature, and there it was, along the lakeshore, waiting for me to finally notice. I suppose it could have been just an unusual natural occurrence, accidentally created by the elements. A mere happenstance. Like the supposed evolution of everything else. But no. Standing there at the edge of Superior, with the evening coolness riding the breeze, there was no doubt in my mind that, like everything else, it had been created with a purpose. I'm not insinuating that it was created by God but by someone who was made in His image. Someone who had a story to tell or an event to commemorate. That evening, I felt a friendship with someone I had never even met.

The next day, we ventured down to the Temperance River. Julie had an inkling to paint there. I had heard that pink salmon should be running in the lower reaches, which gave me an inkling to fish there. We had only visited the Temperance area once before, back when our kids were younger and we first started coming to the north shore. Most of the features upstream from the highway looked familiar. Downstream wasn't familiar at all. It was memorable scenery, so either my memory had a serious gap in it, or we didn't venture downstream the first time we visited. Julie wasn't sure, but I opted to believe we hadn't gone downstream before. Not that it mattered. It just made me feel better not having to think that my memory was on the ropes.

Pink salmon were not in the river yet. That was verified by another fisherman who apparently fished there often. Just before he left, he told me that when the pinks are in you can readily see them from the viewing deck that overlooked the huge bend pool just below the final falls. I took his authoritative word on the matter and climbed back up to the road and beyond.

132

I made a few casting stops between the lower and upper gushing-water gorges, then settled into more serious trout hunting through the extensive boulder field beyond. There, the river was running in thin ribbons between boulders. Wood was non-existent, probably blown out by spring torrents each year. The small holes I infrequently came across didn't offer up anything in the way of fish. Not even small fry poking at my flies. Fortunately, I include pretty water and adventures in my definition of fishing success, so when I decided to turn around and go see how painting was going, I deemed the morning a success and set my sights on a late lunch.

A couple of days later, painting hadn't been going well, so Julie didn't want me around as a witness. She dropped me off at the Brule River, along the Gunflint Trail, and headed on up the Gunflint in search of a worthy scene to paint. I casually ambled my way upstream, more exploring than fishing. The sunny, mild autumn day just felt leisurely. I couldn't help feeling leisurely, too. The pretty little boulder-strewn river I was exploring helped encourage the mood. Good thing, because I couldn't find a fish to save my life. No hits. No follows. No little ones teasing me. Nothing. Multiple flies. Multiple presentations. Numerous locations. Nothing. I suppose I could have been doing something wrong. Maybe multiple things. To remedy the situation, I leisurely blew off those thoughts and relaxed with a snack as I sat on a large boulder, listening to the ramblings of north woods water on its way to Superior.

Later that evening, to satisfy our craving for fish, Julie and I enjoyed the local catch of the day at The Fisherman's Daughter, in Grand Marais. This came with the side benefit of not needing to do any cleaning or cooking. It also came with the side benefit of coleslaw and fries.

The next fall, we were back in the area for the Plein Air Grand Marais painting competition again. It was late afternoon. Julie's first choice of a painting subject—a vibrant patch of Black-eyed Susans with the east break wall and Coast Guard buildings in the background—was already being covered by three other artists. There wasn't a Plan B, so Julie just picked someplace that she liked and had painted the previous year—the Cascades River mouth shoreline. Having already learned that it's best for me not to be present while she's painting, I busied myself poking around the nearby pockets of cobble beach. The pocket beaches in that area are small, so my attention soon transitioned to the river mouth, then naturally progressed upstream. Just above the Highway 61 bridge, I spotted a nice-looking but unfamiliar fish in the shallows. After finding a couple more, I realized they were Pink Salmon. Previously, I had only seen them in pictures, never in the flesh, so it took a minute for my brain to make the identification.

As I explored upstream, fish sightings increased until I was looking over a wider, slower stretch of water with probably fifty or sixty fish in front of me. Not only was nobody fishing, there wasn't even anyone spectating. That was when my plan for the next morning started solidifying. When I shared the great news about fish and a plan with Julie, she didn't seem surprised. Fortunately, she was interested in doing more painting there the next day, so no negotiations were necessary.

The next morning was sunny and cool. Julie's plan, which included going out for breakfast, experienced a setback when we found a sign on the South of the Border Café stating that they were closed on Tuesdays. After a little prodding, Julie's smartphone informed us that the Cascades Lodge Restaurant was open, so I quickly bought my 24-hour non-resident fishing license at Buck's Hardware, and we headed west out of town. It was difficult for me to cross the Cascade River to get to the lodge but not as difficult as it was to eat my breakfast while staring out the window, knowing the river was just out of sight around a slight bend in the road.

When I finally made it to the river at about 9:00 am, I was happy to find the fish were still where I left them the previous evening. The fact that there was nobody else in sight, fishing rod or not, elevated my happiness even more. I had decided not to screw around with waders, so I was wearing quick-dry pants and a scrubby pair of old hiking shoes. I went straight to the spot where I had seen the big collection of fish. There was no change. I tied on a streamer and stepped into the flow. Even though I had plenty of experience wading wet, the briskness of the water came as a slight surprise. I either quickly acclimated to the cold water, or my brain wasn't capable of

134

addressing the water temperature and the fish at the same time, because my focus was soon just on the fish.

After only a few casts, I had a nice male on the line. Unfortunately, he was an accidental catch, snagged on a pectoral fin. I quickly released him and continued casting. Every few casts, I snagged another fish by its fin, but as soon as I saw it wasn't a legitimate catch, I switched directions with my rod to allow the fish to easily pull free.

It took a full hour of casts and retrieves before I finally found a fish agitated enough to strike my fly, resulting in a legal catch. It was a spunky male that made several runs before I was able to bring him in. The tussle momentarily brought me back to my teenage years, catching coho with my dad, but lying at the water's edge was my first Pink Salmon. Up close, his markings were considerably more colorful than I expected. He was downright pretty, in a fishy sort of way. I had decided the previous evening that if I caught a fish or two, they would go on the grill, so I dealt a sharp blow to the head to quickly dispatch the fish. Then I said a brief prayer of thanks and put it on the stringer that I carry in my fishing vest back pouch (but hardly ever use), anchored the other end of the stringer to a heavy rock, and slipped the fish into a shallow pool to keep it cold.

With at least a good start on dinner, I relaxed and began experimenting with other fly patterns. I was sure that an egg simulation would entice some salmon to bite. Good thing I didn't bet on it. The only thing it caught was water and a few snagged rocks. That prompted me to switch to another streamer. During my continued casting and retrieving regimen, I spotted a steelhead and a brightly colored brook trout in the mix of fish. Both were no doubt opportunistically dining. After at least another hour, I legitimately hooked a smaller female salmon. She wasn't as colorful as the male, but she was only about eight feet away when she took my fly, so I was able to witness the strike in detail. The streamer was about six inches from the side of her head, between me and her, when she purposefully turned to the side and struck at the fly three times before she grabbed it. I was so caught up in the unfolding drama, that I almost missed my opportunity to set the hook. Like the male, she too made a few runs for freedom before I was able to bring her in. Also like the male, a quick blow to the head allowed me to add her to the stringer and menu. They were spared from a slow death after spawning, while Julie and I were given the gift of a wild nutritious meal.

With all we needed for a good meal on the stringer, I offered up another thank-you prayer, hooked my fly to an eyelet, and reverted back to a spectator instead of a participant, watching the drama continuing to unfold before me. Still, I had that stretch of river to myself. A few gawkers had come and gone, but nobody else was fishing. Before long, I decided that I should show Julie the gifts we had been given for dinner. As I headed downstream, more people were beginning to arrive. I smiled and politely nodded to each person that I passed. One couple asked if they could take a closer look at the fish, which I readily agreed to. They even wanted to take a picture of me with my catch to show their friends. It felt pretty good bringing home fresh fish for dinner, but I never thought that catching a couple of fish would increase my popularity so much. Fortunately, it didn't increase enough to ever see those pictures show up on the front of a tabloid displayed at a grocery-line checkout.

After letting Julie admire my catch, I tied off the stringer under the bridge, letting our dinner chill in a protected pool, and took a seat on a riverside boulder nearby. From my vantage point, I could keep an eye on the fish while I watched the Cascades flow mingling with Superior waves. As I jotted notes from my time on the river, I expressed another thank-you for the beautiful office I was working in. Intermixed with recording notes were thoughts of fresh salmon cooked on a grill, accompanied by a glass of wine. My north shore office was proving to be a great place to work.

QUIET WATER

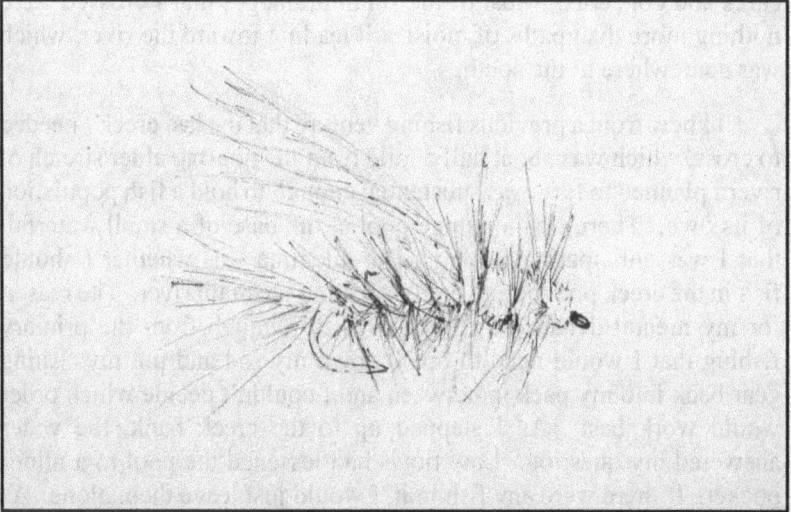

Overnight temperatures had been below fifty degrees Fahrenheit, which is unusual August weather, even here in the Upper Peninsula. With a morning breeze out of the north, the old flannel shirt I was wearing felt comfortable. I did one last mental gear check, locked the truck door, and made my way into the local wilderness area for a much-needed respite from the day-to-day issues that had recently been pummeling me. With my first step away from the road, the quiet water I was heading to began to work its magic of smoothing over the ruts of the previous few weeks. The farther I ventured into the wilderness, the less evident the trail I was following became. As I crossed the second stream that currently wasn't, the trail faded into obscurity, and I began the mile or so of bushwhacking. When I first headed out, I was expecting that I might need my long-sleeve shirt to help ward off biting bugs in addition to the morning chill. That turned out not to be the case. Apparently, the nighttime-turned-morning chill was taking care of holding off the bugs. The morning sun was penetrating the shadowed hardwood forest with cheery patches of light that further helped elevate me above recent cares and concerns. Most of the small drainages that I crossed were nothing more than paths of moist soil leading toward the river, which was somewhere to the south.

I knew from a previous fishing venture that the last creek I needed to cross, which was about half a mile from the non-tag alder stretch of river I planned to fish, was substantial enough to hold a fish population of its own. There was a plunge pool at the base of a small waterfall that I was anticipating fishing. The dilemma was whether I should fish in the creek pool before or after fishing the main river. The reason for my mental debate was that it was far enough from the primary fishing that I would need to break down my rod and put my fishing gear back into my pack in between and I couldn't decide which order would work best. As I stepped up to the creek bank, the water answered my question. Low flows had lessened the pool to a minor pocket. If there were any fish in it, I would just leave them alone. As it usually happens, the view of the waterfall feeding the pocket was blocked by a large cedar tree that had succumbed to the elements since I had last visited and was horizontal instead of vertical. So, I didn't bother getting out my camera for a picture of the falls.

After what seemed like a long bushwhack through blowdowns and muddy seepages, I finally found the main river right at the edge of the tag alder guard. The water was definitely lower than I had hoped, but it was at least still fishable. In front of me were two dark holes that looked like they should hold fish. It was 11:00 am. I wanted to go ahead and eat lunch so that I didn't have to interrupt fishing once I got started. My plan was to find a prime lunch location at the water's edge, but I didn't want to spook any fish. Below the holes was a large log perched right in the edge of the water, but it looked a little precarious for unpacking my daypack without dropping anything, or everything, in the water. My backup plan ended up being a river-view location back in the trees where I could eat, change into my scrub wading shoes (retired hiking shoes), and rig up my rod without losing things in the river or wetting more than my shoes and lower pant legs.

When I got in the water with an attractor fly pattern tied to my tippet, I found the two dark holes to be roughly eight-inch-deep water slowly flowing over bedrock that was covered with a thin film of dark silt. I presented my fly several times just in case, but apparently, nothing was there to notice. In my estimate, the river needed another six inches of water to make those holes viable fish-holding features. As I worked my way upstream, I found the same to be true with most of the runs and would-be holes. They probably would have fished well back in late May. Being anchored in late August as I was, I just made a mental note about potential May fishing and continued exploring my way upstream. Eventually, I found a dark bend hole that was truly a hole. A few submerged logs were vaguely visible near the head of the dark water. Working my way up from the back of the hole, the first several casts simply provided casting practice. Then, near one of the logs, there was a quick hit and run where the fish was off before it was even on. Several casts later, I hooked what I suspected was the same fish. It looked to be about nine inches long, but it shook loose of the hook before I had an opportunity to verify my estimate. Continued casting proved fruitless, as everything in the hole was likely spooked and not interested in participating.

Just around the corner was another bend hole that was significantly larger. After floating my fly across a good share of the hole, an eight-inch brook trout came to hand. It hit just as I was preparing to lift the fly for another cast. I continued fishing that hole for a while longer, but the catching was apparently over. I thought about changing to a different fly, but there was still more fishable water upstream and I had ventured out into the wilderness to explore as much as I was there to fish. Just upstream, in a short run, there was a small trout toying with my fly. I played the game for a few minutes, then continued exploring new water for bigger fish.

While working my way through several shallow riffles and runs, I heard what sounded like a muffled growling sound, which quickly pulled my attention away from fishing. The source of the sound turned out to be the strong wingbeats of a nearby hummingbird that was diligently servicing a patch of brilliant orange streamside flowers. I later regretted not taking a closer look to identify the flowers, but at the time, my attention immediately shifted back to the river and my search for trout. Going by a vague mental image of the flowers, I believe they were Jewelweed, which is known for being a favorite of hummingbirds.

Above the shallow stretch of riffles and runs, I came upon a beaver retreat. There was a new low dam with a more substantial but still relatively new-looking dam at the upstream end of the small impoundment. Beyond the upstream dam, tag alders crowded in from both stream banks. I made a few casts into the impoundment, but casting room was minimal, which I knew meant an increased probability of losing a fly. Risk sometimes comes with a reward but not always. I wimped out and avoided the risk by heading back downstream, intent on running a streamer through the two holes where I had found success earlier.

The hole that had previously produced an eight-inch brook trout yielded two more spunky brook trout to a small streamer. The hole where I had hooked the nine-inch brook trout didn't offer up anything more. I could have, and maybe should have, tried a different fly or two. Maybe the extra effort would have resulted in catching a few more fish. Then again, maybe not. I had enjoyed some quality quiet time in the middle of a designated wilderness area, unbothered and unpressured by other anglers or other cares. It was fishing like fishing should be. Focused, in a relaxed sort of way. It was quiet water time.

By my definition, *quiet water* is not necessarily slow-moving or slack water. It's simply water that I have to myself. It's where I can move and think at my own pace without worrying about someone else moving in or having recently been there. Quiet water means that I'm alone with the stream. It's undisturbed water and undisturbed thoughts. Quiet water means freedom to explore—for fish or anything else.

If a person gets away from easy access points, the likelihood of finding quiet water increases dramatically. That being said, a good share of Upper Peninsula water readily qualifies as quiet water.

I have found that quiet water isn't always productive water—at least not from a fish-catching point of view. Then again, often it is. Seth Waters, owner of Dark Waters Fly Shop and Guide Service in Iron River, says that he regularly targets locations in lonely-looking spaces on the map. Sometimes he does well from a catching standpoint, sometimes not. Knowing Seth, though, I'm sure he always hooks into an adventure.

Small streams are usually quiet and uncrowded, but they don't always need to be small to be non-busy. Depending on when and where you fish, most Upper Peninsula streams typically offer quiet water retreats. Case in point, I was fishing a stream less than a hundred yards from a well-used gravel road, not more than a mile upstream from where it crosses M-28. Access was incredibly easy. My companions were the river, fish, and birds. The few hours that I fished were completely at my own pace.

Even though nothing was hatching at the time, I opted for a dry fly, just because that's what I wanted to fish with. My first several casts were into a large hole with a tiny waterfall at the head. After working my way through the entire hole with not so much as a teasing hit, I cast the same fly to the head of the hole, just below the water falling over the log, and let the fly drown just a bit so it was tumbling just below the surface. Within a couple of seconds, a lively eight-inch brook trout hit it hard and set the hook itself. After releasing that first fish, I moved upstream to fish a moderate-size run. Another eight-inch brookie boldly attacked my fly. This one was obviously a male preparing for the upcoming spawning festivities. It boasted a bright tangerine belly with vivid spots and fin markings.

Continuing upstream, I soon had three more trout on the line for only a few seconds before their antics released them from my hook. There were a couple of holes that I was sure held trout, but they never showed themselves. I probably should have switched to a streamer for the holes, but I was relaxing as much as I was fishing, so I decided to continue exploring my way upstream, enjoying the lack of competition and pressure. I was also enjoying the fact that my casting was going well, and I hadn't lost any flies to trees or submerged logs. A few hours of quiet water had worked its magic once again, as it usually does.

Whether you're fishing or not, quiet water is good for whatever ails you. If you don't have any known ailments, it's good preventative medicine. Regular doses can work wonders. It's far cheaper than doctor-prescribed medications and doesn't come with any side effects. Although, I've found that regular doses of quiet water does usually lead to an addiction, or at least strong yearnings. The good news is that in places like the Upper Peninsula, it's pretty easy to score a fix.

CARP RIVER

After spending a good share of the day in an apartment, I was ready to escape to a river somewhere. Babysitting our granddaughter was fun and rewarding, but I was glad that we were past the apartment-living stage of our lives. I needed to get out beyond the walls. Even though it had been on my list all summer, I had not yet fished the Carp River, near Marquette. I don't recall a specific reason for choosing the location other than it was relatively close and outside of town. My wife, Julie, and I followed the two-track off 553 upstream to the Morgan Falls parking lot, which was a patch of compressed dirt that was big enough for a few small vehicles if everyone parked tight.

The falls are actually in Morgan Creek, maybe ten yards from where the creek flows into the Carp River. Descending the final drop that forms the falls, I was disappointed to see most of the area near the falls and river was bare dirt, obviously caused by an abundance of foot traffic – and probably prolific partying, based on other evidence. The afternoon was winding down, and we were already there, so Julie started setting up her painting easel, intent on painting the falls, minus its bare-dirt banks. I started rigging up my fly rod.

My first casts were right at the creek mouth, where I was plagued by constant snags. I quickly decided that it would be difficult to hook a fish with my fly spending most of its time hooked on rocks and wood. Downstream looked promising, so I waded across the river and down to the first bend. There was no hatch in progress, so having had some previous success with it, I was fishing a #14 pheasant tail nymph. At the end of the sweeping bend was a chute that spilled into a deep run with a log running along its far side. Several passes through the run produced nothing. Then I put the nymph closer to the log and let it run out a bit longer to where it started to swing like a streamer at the end of the drift. During the swing, the line began to dance, and I netted an eight-inch Rainbow. Not big. Not a legal keeper. But a fly-caught trout in a pretty stretch of water, even if it was well visited. The inept feeling from all those initial snags started to fade. That's when I started to relax and scrutinize the river, looking for trout-holding pockets. I began to fish like a hunter.

The water downstream looked fast and rocky, without much for pockets. I'm sure there probably was some holding water there, but it didn't stand out to me at the time. So, I moved back up above the creek inlet and found a moderately deep hole lined with large rocks on the near side. The head of the hole was a fast white chute. The pheasant tail made the journey from the white chute through the dark hole several times, unmolested. As I was preparing to cast again to the head of the hole, something swirled in the edge of visibility. Something large. As I stared, trying to distinguish fact from fantasy, a sleek dark apparition separated from the rest of the darkness and cruised the far side of the hole before fading back in. The #14 nymph hanging from the end of my tippet looked inadequate. I needed the meatiness of a streamer. I thought the fish would agree.

Stepping back away from the hole, I pulled out my small box of streamers and selected one of my favorites. A Mickey Finn. Even with my flip-down magnifier, I couldn't thread the tippet through the eye. On my third frustrated attempt, I noticed the tell-tale glare of glue plugging the hook eye. With time ticking away in my brain, I just grabbed a different fly instead of using something to poke the glue out. The stand-in was a Muddler Minnow. I just wanted to get a fly back in the water.

Easing back out into casting position, I saw the fish-shaped shadow swirl and cruise the outskirts of the hole again. This time it was crisp against a bottom of sandy gravel. A second shadow, darker than the first, followed. Once the two shadows rejoined the darkness of the hole, I flipped the muddler up and across and retrieved it right through the middle of the unknown. Again and again I retrieved the muddler, tingling with anticipation. After a few minutes of quietly standing and staring, I caught a glimpse of another swirl. They were still there. Two roll casts later, a six-inch rainbow came squirming to my net. Not what I was hoping for, but I said a brief thank-you prayer as I was turning it loose, hoping it was just a prelude to a bigger event. Several more times, I pulled the muddler through their lair, but the two fish I was dreaming of never showed themselves again. They sent out another six-inch stand-in, but that rainbow never led to the pot of gold I was visualizing either.

Time was getting short, and I still wanted to take a look at the Carp River Falls, which was a half-mile or more upstream. I reluctantly hooked up the Muddler and headed over to pick up Julie, who was already packing up. Glancing back toward the hole where I assumed the two shadows still lingered, I realized that my outlook had changed. Bigger fish lived in the waters I waded. It wasn't necessarily a revelation, but I now had a mental image to go with the thought.

Farther upstream, the trail to the falls viewing point followed a large aqueduct through the forest. From my recollection, the steel duct was two feet to three feet in diameter. What its original purpose was or who had built it, I had no idea. Its current purpose appeared to be to intrigue people as they hiked out to see the falls. Regardless, it looked like a lot of money and effort to end up as a forgotten relic lying in the forest.

Our first view of the falls was through a small opening in a mature hemlock grove, probably at least a hundred yards away from the churning water. A pair of large trees partially submerged in the foaming roar of water attested to the power we were witnessing. The river was still quite a way down the hill from our vantage point. I had carried in my rod and other fishing gear, just in case, but looking first at the churning falls, then at my watch, I decided it wasn't the day for that venture. I suspected that I would find mostly rainbows below the falls and maybe more brook trout above, but I knew I would need more time to find out. With the thoughts of white water and shadowed fish swirling through my head, we retraced our route along the large steel duct, trying to visualize it in its day. For some reason—probably just reverting back to boyhood—I even climbed up and walked along the top of it for a few minutes. The duct's purpose still eluded me, but those youthful steps felt good anyway.

A year later, again following a morning and early afternoon of babysitting, I was heading back out to just revisit the river near Morgan Falls. Our daughters were taking my wife out for a birthday dinner, so I had some time to use up while they were out. I don't recall if it was just a girl's dinner and I wasn't invited, or if I uninvited myself in order to go fishing. Either way, I had a little time to fish the Carp while we were in the area anyway. The two-track to Morgan Falls ended up being blocked off due to a washout from recent heavy rains. Based on my estimate of walking time, I figured I would only have about fifteen minutes to fish if I chose to haul my fishing stuff in on foot. That didn't sound like it would be worth the effort, but then I reasoned that I had time to kill anyway. Knowing that only fifteen minutes of fishing wouldn't actually happen, I settled on the compromise of making the hike to check out the situation without my fishing gear so that I wouldn't be tempted to fish for a couple of hours and end up in the doghouse. Besides, a glimpse of the river through the trees indicated that the rain that caused the washout still had the river running deeper and faster than normal, so fishing wouldn't likely be worthwhile anyway. Partway to the falls, I passed a younger guy carrying a fly rod on his way out. I couldn't help but ask. He said he had only fished for a short time with no results other than a wet fly. That made me feel better about my decision.

It turned out that the river was indeed running deeper and faster than normal. The holes I had previously fished were fast and murky. I was standing at the mouth of Morgan Creek, wondering if salmon had made it that far upstream yet on their spawning run, when I spotted three relatively small ones in the shallows. It appeared to be two males and a female because two of the fish were obviously working on deciding which one of them had to leave in order to make a pair. I watched two of the fish fight their way up through a fast chute with part of their backs protruding from the water, then lost track of them in the wider white water above. I never did locate them again, but it was getting to be time for me to leave anyway. As I climbed up around Morgan Falls, I was just slightly wishing I had brought my fishing stuff, but then I thought about the doghouse and decided I was better off without the temptation. I headed back to my truck in a light drizzle, carefully eyeing the clear shallows below the falls.

The next time I came back, intent on exploring some of the water between Morgan Falls and the Carp River Falls, I found the road closed to facilitate reconstructing the washout that had previously stymied my fishing plans. Not wanting to turn the rainy afternoon into a hiking trip again instead of a fishing outing, I found a wide enough section of two-track to get my truck turned around and headed back out to the main road. Before pulling out onto the pavement, I scrutinized what I could see of the river at the road crossing and decided that it looked like a better option than spending time driving somewhere else. It was rocky and swift, but there were enough pockets to convince me to go ahead and rig up my rod.

It had been a while since I had managed to carve out some time to fish, so it was refreshing just to be playing in moving water again. The entire stretch I fished was less than a hundred yards, right near the main road. Being immersed in the sights and sounds of the flow, though, it still felt like wild north woods water. Through the course of an hour or so, three small rainbows of about eight inches came dancing to my net. One bolted out from under a protective tree branch and literally did a short tail dance across the stream's surface before restlessly waiting in the net to be released. Amid a rash of busyness and personal uncertainty, that brief connection with the wild was the therapy that I needed to help me resynch. It was an answer to prayer.

147

Eventually, the road was closed to motorized vehicles altogether, which added a twenty-minute hike to reach Morgan Creek. The hike in was an uneventful stroll along a well-maintained two-track meant primarily for mountain bikes. Even though Morgan Falls still tends to be a popular destination, evidenced by the amount of hard-packed bare earth around it, it was devoid of other people when I arrived at 9:30 in the morning. I began fishing just upstream from the creek mouth, where a nice hole was the last time I visited. River dynamics had changed the hole to more of a minor run than a legitimate hole. After a few fruitless casts, I moved on to explore new water. Being that I rarely fish streams with major hatches—or at least I don't tend to fish them during major insect hatches—I often fish with just attractor patterns, nymphs, or streamers. Working my way upstream, I chose a topwater attractor. My second stop was a minor run, surrounded by shallower fast water that flowed through a collection of small boulders. The remains of a fallen tree lay in the shallow water between the bank and the run I was interested in. The obstruction was less than waist-high, so I made my first cast over the tree while I stood at the water's edge. My line began dancing to the tune of an energetic little rainbow. The best way to land it ended up being to quickly lift it over the branches into a small pool that was near the bank. A few seconds later, the fish darted through the branches, back into the run. I hooked my fly to an eyelet and ventured farther upstream to another run that was on the far side of a large boulder. After three or four trips through the back half of the run, there was a silver flash in the run and my fly came out attached to the lip of an eight-inch rainbow. After a couple more quick hits without the fish getting hooked, the fish in the back half of the run appeared to be done with that fly offering. The front half was guarded by the boulder and other assorted large rocks. I'm not sure at what point a large rock begins being classified as a boulder, so I won't worry about it here. I was pretty sure that I could have caught at least one more fish there if I had taken the time to change flies, but I still had more new water to explore, so minimal fly changes were my plan.

Soon, I was into milder flows with more holding water. River access, however, was declining, which often made casting my dry fly a little difficult. That was where I decided on a change of flies and shifted to a small streamer. My first cast down and across the current, letting the fly swing into the main run, brought a ten-inch rainbow to hand, followed soon after by another one a bit smaller.

Farther upstream, a long run was bisected by a large white pine trunk suspended two feet above the river. Fishing from near the head of the run, I let my streamer swing into position under the shelter of the suspended log. A nine-inch rainbow accepted my invitation. A few casts later, an eight-inch brook trout followed suit. In between landing and releasing the two fish, there was a short tussle with flashing silver in the same size range, but I never had an opportunity to touch that fish.

As I continued exploring upstream, the banks quickly gained height and steepness, eventually turning into what I would call a small canyon. At one point, I left my bird's-eye view of the river from atop the ridge and scrambled down to the water's edge between two waterfalls, each only a few feet tall. Two more healthy rainbows came out of the dark water between the falls. A few additional quick hits told me that the two fish I caught were not the only residents of that stretch.

Continuing upstream, water velocity increased, as did the number and height of the falls. The river became more conducive to photography than fishing. I knew the main falls were not much farther upstream, but I also suspected the fishing possibilities were likely not going to improve as I closed in on the falls. I recalled seeing the falls from a distance a few years earlier. Seeing the plunge from a much closer vantage point was tempting, but I had a commitment early in the evening, and I wanted to swing the streamer through some of the faster water down near where I had started fishing. Additional fishing won out over pure sightseeing, and I began the trek back toward the Morgan Creek confluence. Along the way, I was granted the fun of catching a couple more rainbows. Both quickly darted back into the flow as soon as I opened my hand.

When I reached Morgan Creek, the well-used gathering area was no longer unoccupied. Besides a few bicyclists and a couple of motorcycle riders who were not supposed to be there, the crew included a family of four that was swimming in the Morgan Falls plunge pool. That ended my plan to fish the plunge pool before I left. Instead, I swung the little streamer through a small run right where the creek and river join forces. A few swings later, one last rainbow came thrashing to my hand. I packed up my gear and prepared for the hike to my truck as the two kids splashed into the plunge pool. The dad was spectating from the top of the falls. Mom was taking a more leisurely approach, watching the kids as she lay on her side atop the picnic table. As I passed by the dad on my way out, we both smiled in acknowledgment of our good day on the river.

THE DEAD

I had never fished the Dead River, but it was on my "to fish" list, primarily due to author Jerry Dennis once noting that he thought the Dead was likely named by a fisherman in an effort to keep other people away. So, when my friend Jim asked if I wanted to go fishing and included the Dead as a possibility, I decided to take him up on it. I knew the river had likely changed since Jerry's description due to the scouring by a watery bulldozer resulting from a dam burst some fifteen years ago, but it would still be new water for me regardless. The day was sunny and quickly warming as I stepped out of the truck, looking forward to taking the Dead on its current merits, whatever they might be. We walked the last fifty yards to the river through a floodplain of tamarack and coreopsis flowers, probably planted as part of the original cleanup after the dam burst incident. There wasn't much shade on the water, but it looked clean and healthy. I should have thought to check the water temperature, but my mind was focused on finding fish. In hindsight, it had been an unusually cool summer, so a temperature issue was unlikely anyway.

Jim left me to start fishing at the first hole we saw when we approached the river, as he meandered off downstream. I was glad because the hole looked like trout water. With no hatch in progress, I started off with my favorite yellow stimulator, which, coincidently, Jim had given me on an earlier fishing venture. I don't think I've ever been skunked using that fly, so I cast it with confidence. Many times, I cast it with confidence. Nobody was interested. I reluctantly moved upstream to a collection of riffles, knowing I was leaving behind some trout. The same story unfolded there, whether I fished the stimulator dry or wet. Not a hit. Heading off downstream looking for some takers, I covered a hundred yards of good-looking trout water without being able to coax anything out of their dark hideouts.

When I worked my way around Jim, he had already caught a few brookies on a red squirrel tail streamer. He had given me a couple before we left the vehicle, so I decided to use my new flip-focal magnifier to tie one on before we ate our lunch. Just prior to my last fishing outing, my old flip-down magnifier had broken, so I tried just using my reading glasses, which don't provide much magnification. It took about ten minutes for me to get my tippet through the eye of the hook. That prompted the purchase of the new flip-focal magnifier. After lunch, the first riffle I fished gave up three nice brook trout to my new fly. At about seven, eight, and nine inches, they weren't lunkers, but they were certainly healthy, feisty, and beautiful trout. Something about catching that first fish of the day just seems to put me at ease. Not that I was tense prior to catching that fish, but I definitely felt more relaxed afterward. Once I catch that first fish, others seem to come more easily. It's like something resets in my head and everything just flows smoother. Within the next fifty yards, two more trout came to my net. One that was about nine inches long came up after the fly with such spunk that after it grabbed the fly just below the surface, its momentum carried its entire body out of the water. After a short tussle, that fish managed to transfer the fly to my net, which required some effort and magnification to work free.

The next leapfrog move around Jim put me back in the river just above a dark bend run. My second cast into the dark water brought out a nice brookie for me to admire. Several casts later, a plump nine-inch fish followed suit. That one snagged the fly on my net while it was still attached to the fish, which made for some tricky unhooking.

That's happened several times, sometimes making me seriously consider getting a new net with heavy-duty rubbery netting instead of a braided net. The main thing holding me back from a new net is that I simply don't like the looks of them. That, and the fact that I hate replacing something that technically works. I guess neither are good reasons for continuing to use my old net, but I still do. Besides the net ordeal, that second spunky fish also ravaged my fly. The red squirrel tail streamer was minus the squirrel tail, as well as the shiny body. It was just a hook with a few ratty-looking red fibers loosely attached. I retired it to the drying patch on my fishing vest—not that there was much to dry—and tied on the second red squirrel tail that I had. Not far downstream, another feisty fish took my new fly and made it look old. I decided that it looked more crippled than dead, so instead of changing to a different fly, I continued fishing with the beat-up one. I did end up having to clip it off and retie it because my line somehow ended up going through my net and I didn't think I could weave it back through without completely ruining the fly or re-snagging it on the net mesh.

Apparently, I was right about the fly still being useful, because I caught one more brookie just downstream. After that, there was a small waterfall, followed by fast water and snot-slippery shale going into a short-walled canyon. All the shale bedrock was nearly impossible to stand up or walk on. A fishing attempt in a pocket just below the falls proved that fact to me. Fortunately, a wet left sleeve was the only damage done.

We bushwhacked around some of the fast water, but Jim and I both ended up somewhat stranded amid fast water and slimy rocks, with more of the same stretching to the next bend, some hundred yards downstream. After checking the time and factoring in the drive home, we decided it was time to start bushwhacking our way back to Jim's 4-Runner anyway. Back at the vehicle, I couldn't resist swinging the red squirrel tail through the first hole that I fished with the yellow stimulator, so I walked back over to the river. High on anticipation, I made several retrieves through the hole, thinking there had to be a trout in there somewhere. If there was, it wasn't any more interested in the small streamer than the stimulator. Obviously, we were done. I clipped off my fly and hooked it to the drying patch on my vest. It felt satisfying to get out on new water and catch some fish. It also felt good to get out of the steamy neoprene waders. They are definitely more enjoyable to wear in cooler conditions. Had I known we wouldn't have any muck or deep water to deal with, I would have just waded wet, which is my normal mode of operation in the summer. Regardless, we at least didn't have mosquitoes to deal with and I only had to endure two deer fly bites. I had personal encounters with several healthy brook trout, and I think Jim had a few more than I did. It was a good day out in the U.P. wilds getting to know The Dead.

The following week, I had an opportunity to try a different section of the river, downstream from the reservoir. Access included about a mile hike, part of which was a bushwhack through the woods. Most of the hike was in the rain, which seemed odd because there were no clouds above me. They were farther north, over Lake Superior. I wasn't concerned about getting wet because I was going to be wading wet anyway. I just didn't like the rain because it was starting to wash off my bug spray. Regardless, typical for August, mosquitoes were few and far between, which I appreciated because tying on flies while wearing a bug net has proven to be an issue. It's also difficult to see in the water with a bug net, even with polarized glasses. Based on previous experience, I left my rod broken down for the hike in and just attached the reel to the butt end to reduce the number of things I had to carry or potentially drop. By the time I reached the river, the small thunderstorm had cleared, and the sun was sparkling off the water.

Stepping into the river in a rock-strewn section, I began casting the yellow stimulator I had selected to a small run between boulders. Within the first few casts, I had a quick hit that caught me with a little too much slack in my line to set the hook before the fish was free and gone. I considered having a fish on so soon to be a good sign, even if it was only for a few seconds. Just upstream, in a similar run, I managed to land a plump eight-inch brook trout. After removing the hook, the feisty fish darted back into the run before I completely opened my hand. Continuing upstream, the next trout, which was slightly smaller, took my fly just above a pointed rock that was protruding from the water, and darted toward the center of the river, wrapping my line around the rock. Fortunately, I was able to flip my line over the rock before the fish pulled loose. After releasing that brookie, I saw what looked like a much bigger fish aggressively take a natural bug from the surface near a lone rock. I moved a little closer and began casting to that fish, or at least to where I thought that fish might be. A few casts later, a seven-inch stand-in took my fly just as aggressively. The trout I was catching might not have been big, but they were certainly energetic.

There was a short fishless stretch after that. Well, a short catchless stretch is probably more appropriate. I'm pretty sure there were some fish mixed in there somewhere. I just didn't catch them. Then I began casting to a sunny riffle with diamond sparkles on the water. It was under the edge of a sparsely foliated overhanging yellow birch. My first catch there was a small brook trout. It was too pretty of a place to walk away from after only a few casts, so I continued casting into the magazine-photo scene. My second catch in that location was the birch. The intercepting branch was too high to reach, and the fly was too tangled to retrieve with my rod tip. Even though the twig was thin, it proved to be stronger than my 4x tippet. The liberated fly had been working pretty well, so I tied on another of the same and set my sights farther upstream, where the river split around a small rocky island. The side branch rejoined the main flow through a cascading waterfall about four feet tall. Just upstream from the bottom of the cascade, the main channel included a relatively deep run that I was sure held fish, or at least *a* fish. The best casting location to fish the run was in the bottom of the cascade. So, I caught my next brookie while standing in the middle of the cascading waterfall, which made me feel like I was fishing in some exotic location. The spunky nine-inch male sported a tangerine sunset belly and neon side spots. It looked like it was coloring up for spawning even though it was only early August. I had a hard time imagining that he would be able to get any more colorful than he already was, but I opened my hand to let him give it a try. Nothing else came from the run, but I couldn't ask for more anyway.

Above the cascade and around a bend, the side branch flowed through a massive logjam. Below the jam was a dark pool. I was surprised when my first several casts into the pool produced nothing. Then a small trout of about six inches darted from the dark to grab my fly. Several casts later, its twin was dancing on the end of my line. After that, I moved on around the logjam and rejoined the main channel where it spread out into a wide dark hole below a churning waterfall. I floated the yellow stimulator in several locations across the dark water without seeing even a hint of a fish. At that point, I decided it was time to switch to a streamer, which I would probably want to do for the trip back downstream anyway. Even though the fly was different, the results were the same. It was a picturesque location, so I eventually just stood there on a flat boulder for a bit and watched the river. Nothing was hitting the surface like I had seen in several locations on my journey upstream, so I resumed offering the streamer. The fish continued ignoring it. Maybe I just didn't get it close enough to a fish to get an interaction. I envisioned the area I was fishing to be the type of place where fish cruised instead of holding in a small zone. It looked like big-fish water to me, so I was tempted to linger and keep trying. In the back of my mind, though, I knew there was more new water to explore downstream. I also knew it would soon be getting into the heat of the afternoon and I still had a long warm hike back to my vehicle.

My mental tug-of-war ended with me working my way back downstream, swinging the streamer as I went. I caught a nice brookie from one of the runs that I had caught a fish from on my journey upstream. That turned out to be the only action for my streamer that day, though. Nothing came from any of the other runs or riffles. Down past my starting point, I had high hopes for a shaded run and a dark bend hole, but nothing was interested in my streamer offering. Switching back to a dry fly didn't change things. I was getting into a stretch of river with mostly slower water and a series of holes. Most of it would likely not be wadable. The early afternoon was full sun and warm, verging on hot. I clipped off my fly, broke down my rod, and waded back across to where I needed to be to begin the warm hike out. As I snaked my way through the shaded woods, I came to the conclusion that Jerry's speculation about The Dead just might contain some truth.

THE LAST DAY

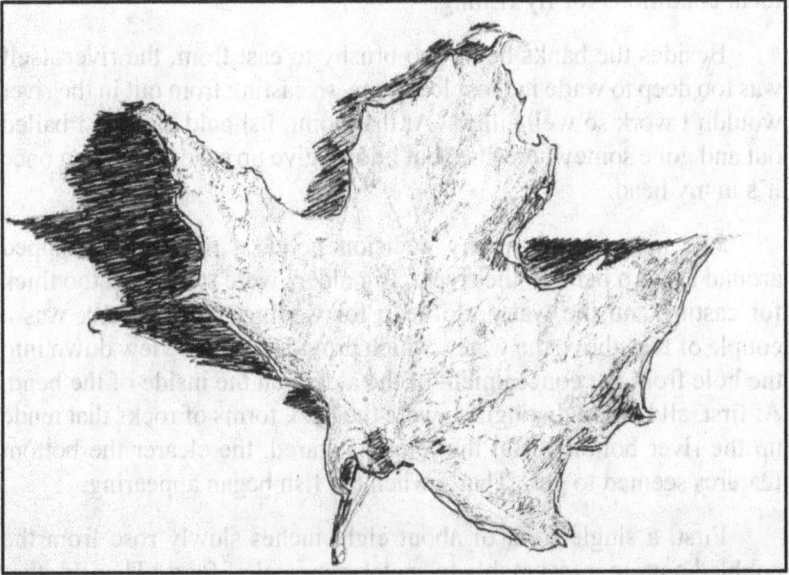

When it comes to things you enjoy, the end is always difficult. The last day of a family vacation. The last day that you live in a home where you raised your family. And, when you're a kid, the last day of summer break.

It was the last day of the regular trout season, which to me often seems like it comes almost immediately after the first day of trout season. I decided to fish someplace close to home so as not to waste a lot of time just driving. The closest reliable place I knew of was the Rock River. The mouth was only ten minutes from my house and one of the stretches that I liked to fish was only another ten minutes upstream. Even though I didn't want a long drive, I still felt like doing something different. So, I opted for fishing a section of the river I had not fished before. The stretch that intrigued me on the plat map required a short bushwhack to reach the river. That, and my experience with other stretches of that river, should've been my first clue that the area I picked would be thick and brushy—not the most ideal conditions for fly fishing.

Besides the banks being too brushy to cast from, the river itself was too deep to wade in most locations, so casting from out in the river wouldn't work so well either. At that point, I should have just bailed out and gone somewhere else, but I don't give up easily on a plan once it's in my head.

Just upstream from my decision point, a nice hole wrapped around a sharp bend in the river. Tag alders were still much too thick for casting and the water too deep for wading, but the bank was a couple of feet above the water, which provided a good view down into the hole from the concealment of the alders on the inside of the bend. At first, all I could distinguish were the hazy forms of rocks that made up the river bottom. But the longer I stared, the clearer the bottom features seemed to get. That's when the fish began appearing.

First, a single trout of about eight inches slowly rose from the cobbled bottom, presumably to snatch a morsel of food. Then another trout of similar size rose from a different location. A third fish soon appeared, then a fourth. The last one looked to be a little more than a foot long. That one had my attention as I tried to figure out how to get a fly to it. Mentally, I found myself landing that fish before I even had a fly in the water. After forcing myself to just watch for a bit, I finally concluded that I needed to be on the other side of the river where there was a slight opening that just might allow for a cast of sorts.

After backing away from the water as stealthily as I could, I worked my way upstream, crossed the river well above the hole, and made my way through the woods back down to the small opening on the outside of the bend. The opening wasn't as roomy as it looked from the other side of the river. Even though I managed to make a few awkward casts, I couldn't quite get the bead-head nymph to where it needed to be to entice a fish. Roll casting didn't even seem to be working for that spot. I had learned the hard way in other similar situations that trying to force the issue usually leads to a fly hanging in a tree somewhere. To protect my fly investment, I decided to move on upstream in search of a different end-of-the-season trout.

The one I found was in an even more difficult spot to fish. I watched it through a small gap in the streamside foliage as I quietly ate my lunch. The fish was holding steady above a large flat rock, highlighted in full sunlight. When it rolled on its side to pick something off the rock, exposing a silvery side with a pale pink stripe and reddish gill plates, I could clearly identify it as a rainbow.

Several other trout of various sizes were visible farther upstream, all predictably in difficult places to fly fish. In addition, any little noise sent them dashing for cover. As I was watching one fish from an alder hideout, I moved my foot and accidentally crunched a small stick. The trout, which was close to twenty feet away, immediately peeled away from the rock it was holding near and bolted downstream.

When my explorations reached a section of river with shallow water and not many fish-holding features, there was also an easy exit to the road, so I reluctantly took it and strolled toward my truck. My leisurely pace was to keep from overheating in the flannel shirt that had felt so good earlier in the morning but wasn't needed in the afternoon heat. I wasn't exactly hot, but I didn't want to get hot either. I hated going home without catching a fish, but things were just not working out well.

On the way home, I drove slowly, with the truck window down to take in the autumn air. Colors weren't very eye-catching yet, but the herbal fragrance of fall was unmistakably there.

Later, while I was tinkering at home, the thought of giving up started bothering me. Even though some rivers would still be open to trout fishing after the clock struck midnight, I was feeling an urgency to catch one last fish before the regular season ended.

With only a couple of hours of daylight remaining, I chose an un-named creek less than two miles from home for my last attempt. Shadows were heavy on the dark water when I reached the confluence where the little creek joined the Laughing Whitefish River. The water wasn't deep, but I hoped the few small holes not far from the mouth would be holding some fish—or at least one.

They did. The hole at the first bend produced a small rainbow trout on the second cast. It took the same red Copper John I had been using earlier in the day. Even though it wasn't big enough to be a legal fish, it somehow made me feel better. It wasn't exactly a fish to brag about, but it was a fish. More importantly, it was a trout. Sometimes it doesn't take much to tip the emotional scale to the success side. A few more small trout came to hand that evening, but the first one felt the best and set a relaxed mood for the waning minutes of the season that night. I had finally fished the creek that had caught my eye almost a year earlier when we had first moved to the area. Successfully even. There was still more water upstream, but I had done what I came to do. It was getting dark enough to make it difficult to see exactly where I was casting anyway. A few exposed rocks cradled a collection of semi-colored maple leaves that looked bright against the dark rocks and water. The evening chill was settling in but not enough to warrant rolling down my flannel sleeves. I took a deep breath of autumn air and followed the little creek back down to the river trail that would lead me home.

The last day of trout season isn't always a struggle, but like the last day of anything, it tends to get your mind working. I remember one last day being full sun and shirt-sleeve warm. I was lamenting a bit over the lack of trout fishing I had done that season. It was the tail-end of the COVID-19 fiasco, which here in the Upper Peninsula didn't really amount to much as far as I was concerned. It certainly did affect things, but it wasn't the cause of my lack of fishing. At the beginning of that trout season, I was inspired by a local Trout Unlimited presentation and had promised myself that I would fish at least once each week throughout the season. Well, it only took three or four weeks for my big plans to start falling apart. Bugs, weather, water temperature, busy schedule—there was no lack of reasons or excuses. The result was that I simply didn't get out fishing nearly as much as I had planned, which in hindsight, isn't all that unusual.

I don't recall if it was me or my buddy Jim who suggested we spend the last day up on the Yellow Dog. Either way, there was no real discussion. We just went. When we reached the river at about 10:30 am, we both tied on one of the yellow stimulators that Jim likes to tie. He left me to make the first cast as he made his way upstream. After snagging on a log, I got a hard hit in the first hole in a sharp tree-filled bend. Jim caught six small fish just upstream as I was working on getting my head screwed on straight so that I could do a decent job of fishing.

I leap-frogged around Jim and promptly caught a beautiful male brook trout about eight inches long. His belly was sunset orange—the deep burning orange that comes late in the sunset, near the horizon. That was when I stopped counting fish, and I think Jim did too. There was no goal. No competition. No big expectations. We were just two friends sharing a wild U.P. river on a gorgeous autumn day, fishing. Actually, I would have to say that what we were doing was not even fishing. We were fishin'. Relaxed and informal, just like fishin' should be.

I used the same fly most of the time we were there. I lost it once when I made a short bushwhack around Jim to avoid spooking fish, but I managed to find it hanging on a small spruce limb. Eventually, I lost the fly in a jumble of sticks at the head of a hole. I tried digging through the tangle to find it, but I quickly decided that it wasn't worth impaling a finger for. So, I tied on one of the other yellow stimulators Jim had given me and proceeded with my explorations.

By the time we decided to leave, I'm guessing that Jim and I had each caught roughly twenty fish. We'd also hooked, if only for a second, about as many more. Most were in the six- to eight-inch range. A couple may have gone nine inches, and I had teases by a couple of trout that looked to be about a foot in length. Some hit the fly on the surface. Others didn't touch it until it had drowned a little. Overall, we fished for about six hours, according to my watch, but it didn't seem like anywhere near that long. I wanted to continue, but I needed to get home to put the cap on my truck and pack up for a family cabin weekend.

On the long walk back to Jim's vehicle, we saw lots of deer tracks and flushed a grouse. What we didn't see was other people. Other than a few boot prints from previous visitors, there wasn't a sign of other people roaming the river. The water was ours to enjoy. It was a good day of fishin'. In fact, it was just a good day. Period. Like you hope every day on the water is.

On the last day of any trout season, I always expect that I'll be out fishing on a stream somewhere. When plans completely fall apart because of weather or some other fact of life, I feel a tinge of regret for not getting out somewhere. Anywhere. Trout season ending as fall colors are seriously ramping up complicates my decision-making as I'm trying to decide what to do when, all the time fearing I will miss out on something regardless of what I decide to do. I know all too well that soon rainy breezy days will hasten the falling of fall. There is an empty feeling in my gut as autumn and trout season are both slipping away minute by minute. At times like this, life feels like it's just a short series of high-speed moments that are gone before you really experience them.

When I find myself getting anxious about the closing of trout season and the acceleration of autumn, I try to pack as much life into each day as I can—as I really should do every day anyway—and I try to savor the moments that I have. I also remind myself that even though I'm lamenting the loss of some seasons, the season for dreaming, scheming, and planning future forays is always open. So, I begin preparations for next season. For me, what connects the end of one trout season to the beginning of the next is a parade of good books and hot tea intermingled with deep thoughts, red wine and writing journals. And of course, mental replays of highlights from seasons past. Sometimes the replays are slightly altered from their original form but, as long as they're for my own viewing, that's my prerogative.

SIGNIFICANCE

Outdoors pursuits and environmental concerns tend to go hand-in-hand. Especially these days. Fishing is no exception. Based on news clips, weather forecasts, magazine articles, scholarly papers, and sometimes just a casual look out the window, our climate seems to be on a rampage. Depending on which media source you choose, you can read about severe drought conditions stressing some of our western states at the same time that historically high Lake Superior water levels are driving unprecedented shoreline erosion. The monster that was once called Global Warming has now been reborn as Climate Change and new waves of invasive species seem to be sweeping in on us on a regular basis. The duo of climate change and invasive species are roaming the world like twin Godzillas, stomping on our hapless environment and natural resources.

Every conservation organization, environmental group, and outdoors-loving person seems to be involved in a project to somehow counter the attack. I'm no exception. Planting trees, for instance, to shade streams, stabilize ground, and absorb carbon. Or generally intervening to help landscapes and wildlife be more resilient. And it's probably no surprise that many of the initiatives that I am personally involved in are focused on aiding and preserving trout. Primarily brook trout.

During this crusade, I read a thought-provoking article in the August 2021 issue of Acts & Facts Magazine. The article focused on brook trout in the Jabez Branch, which is a tributary of the Severn River in Maryland. Due to multiple factors (most of which are likely human induced), the stream was becoming too warm to support a viable brook trout population. In the article, author James Johnson posed the question, "Should a freshwater stream be restored to make it habitable for a failing fish population such as brook trout?" The premise behind Johnson's question was that it made sense that Creationists would proactively care about biodiversity and environmental stewardship, but why should Evolutionists care? Well, even though it's an interesting question, I'm not looking to start a heated argument. So, I'm not going to wade into the Creation versus Evolution debate, but I *will* simply share my thoughts from the standpoint of a firm believer in Creation.

It seems to me that losing a certain species of fish would just be a normal part of the evolutionary process. These losses would just be part of what is often called survival of the fittest or natural selection. Something else, like maybe brown trout, would just take over the environmental niche once occupied by brook trout, and the evolutionary process would continue on. Or, somehow, some of the local brook trout would adapt to the new conditions and begin a brook trout transformation as part of the evolutionary process.

Actually, the question goes far beyond just brook trout, or even fish. Losing a certain species of fish, animal, tree, or anything, would just be part of the evolutionary process and shouldn't be a concern. As long as we human beings make the cut and are still here, who cares? If everything that inhabits the earth is nothing more than a chance happenstance or the result of an accidental occurrence, then nothing should really have any importance. That includes us. If human beings are nothing more than a quirky blink in the evolutionary eons, then we really don't matter and neither does anything else. So, who cares about a particular species of fish disappearing from a particular stream?

Well, I care. And so does a sizeable portion of humanity. It's a matter of significance. The fact that everything in this world—everything in this universe for that matter—has its own special place, its own niche that only it fits and functions in, means that everything has a special role. From my perspective, everything was created with a special purpose. Everything has significance, from microbes to whales, and grains of sand to galaxies. And it seems like our significance and the significance of everything around us is a pretty universal understanding, regardless of what that belief is based on.

That significance is what makes life, life. It is what makes every moment worth living. In fact, it is what makes every moment possible. It's what relationships are built on and why we need those relationships. It's why we miss people and things when they are gone. Those people and things are not only significant to us, but they are also significant in the grand scheme of a living world and an interconnected cosmos. Each piece of the Creation masterpiece matters. The significance and importance of our natural world—our home—is programmed into us as human beings. Not by eons of evolution, but because we were created to be an integral part of that natural world. In fact, we were designated to be caretakers of that natural world.

Significance is why our interactions with other people and other living things often feel magical. And so it is with those other living beings that we call trout. I'm attracted to their elusiveness and the magical feel of my personal encounters with their vibrance. After the personal interaction with a wild trout, each time I opened my hand and the scales and the fins and the flesh darted back into the flow, the magic didn't go. It stayed, gently held in my mind, even though I couldn't fully grasp it or define it. The magic lingered. Even today, the magic of a thousand moments swims the streams of my mind. In the watershed of life known only to me, encounters with fur and feathers and fins intermingle with family and friends. They flow through mountain vistas, deep forests, flowered meadows, wilderness lakes, tents, cabins, and homes. It's a natural collection of seemingly unrelated moments held together by faith. A faith that goes beyond the limits of this world and gives those experiences significance and meaning.

Looking at the interconnectedness and interdependence of everything in our world and out into the surrounding universe, I don't see a hodgepodge collection of chance occurrences or evolutionary byproducts. I see a purposeful system, designed to work exactly as it does, with each piece in its designated place. Each piece, from grand to miniscule, has a purpose, and from that purpose comes significance.

So, does it matter if a certain species of fish disappears from a certain stream where it once naturally existed? Should we be concerned with taking care of and being good stewards of the world that we are an integral part of? Absolutely! Everything that was created to be part of the world we were given to live in is important. It has significance. And so does everyone in the long ancestral line of humanity. The entire roughly six thousand years of it.

Looking at fish, what if whatever is lost is artificially replaced by something else? For instance, in the issue with the Jabez Branch, what if more tolerant brown trout were introduced into the stream to replace the failing brook trout population? What if that scenario was repeated until brook trout in many of their strongholds joined Michigan grayling on the list of what once was?

Or, for another larger example, when lake trout populations experienced a serious decline in the Great Lakes due to sea lamprey predation, they were supplemented with other salmonoid species. Coho, chinook, pink, and Atlantic salmon, along with brown trout, steelhead, and engineered splake have been introduced over the years to fill the gap left by dwindling lake trout or simply to create additional sport fishing opportunities. Have these changes turned out to be good ideas? Well, it's hard to say. There are certainly some benefits when it comes to fishing opportunities. Unfortunately, there also seems to be mounting evidence that there are some negative effects as well. Like food chain alterations and disruptions, as well as splake crossbreeding diluting lake trout and coaster brook trout gene pools. I'm not going to attempt to expound upon the details because I'm not a trained fisheries biologist, but I will say that when we mess with the design of the world and alter significant pieces of that design, the implications are usually significant as well. More often than not, the implications are significantly detrimental.

A big question that this whole discussion raises is that with people being an integral part of the natural world, when we move other natural things around and deposit them in new locations or when we decide to re-engineer one thing or another, is that considered part of a natural process? Or is that just part of our inherited sinful nature that regularly pops up and causes us to screw things up? I tend to think it's the latter. Humans have a long track record of doing things that are not good for the planet or for other human beings. It's a trend that goes all the way back to when our original ancestors were evicted from the Garden of Eden.

Before I go any further, I should probably make it clear that I have nothing against brown trout, rainbow trout, or various salmon species. In fact, I don't even have any issues with splake. Or at least I don't hold any serious grudges against them.

So, where do we draw the line for moving creatures around to suit our whims, or bioengineering new creatures to replace or augment existing ones? I don't know. Those are bigger questions with broader implications than I am able to wrap my limited brain around. I think the key is to focus on what we already have. We've been given everything we need to survive and function in this world that we live in. In fact, better than just surviving and functioning, we have been graciously given everything we need to prosper in this world. From the standpoint of living beings and organisms, we already have everything that's needed for this world to miraculously function the way it was designed to function. Every piece already exists or will be born into being at its appointed time in the natural process of events that was set in motion at the beginning of time. Just to be perfectly clear, I am not talking about theorized evolutionary processes or random events here. I'm talking about God's purposeful plan.

Our job is to do our best to care for the world we have been given, to be good stewards of the resources and other living creatures that we share this earth with, and to work with other human beings for the common good of all of us. And this is something that I hope we can all come together for, regardless of our individual beliefs.

As for those declining brook trout in the Jabez Branch and other creatures facing similar pending demise, let's intervene to balance the scale before they slip off the edge. Let's do what we can to help right humanity's past wrongs and maintain the delicate natural balance that sustains life on planet Earth, the home that was gifted to all of us. We need to accept the fact that we are not gods and go back to the original plan of working together to care for everything around us that was created by, and still belongs to, the one that is God. The fact that He specifically and specially created each piece of this unfathomable working universe attests to the significance of every piece. I truly think that disregarding that significance would be a significant mistake.

MAGIC
AT THE END OF THE LINE

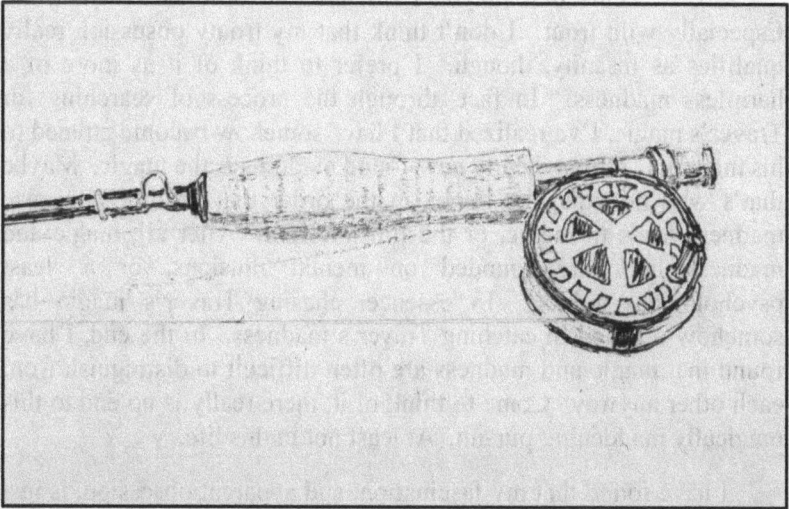

I set out chasing Traver's magic, intent on the notion that I could someday catch it. In that process of chasing, I found myself looking for holding water—and imagining what it might be holding—in every ribbon of moving water I encountered. Even in flowing ditches. Wading through thigh-deep, crusted snow to wet a line on opening day of trout season. Reading trout fishing books, new and obscure alike. Dreaming of fishing adventures as I followed blue lines on maps with my finger. I found myself in a state of heightened anticipation with each cast, often decorating trees well before Christmas. And I've frequently found myself hanging around with other semi-sane individuals with the same affliction.

I always assumed these things were driven by a passion for trout and trout fishing. It has been pointed out to me, though, that passion and obsession can easily be mistaken as the same driving force. Referring to my thesaurus, for passion it notes *Passion – desire, infatuation*. Whereas for obsession, it states *Obsession – preoccupation, fixation, compulsion. See Insanity*.

So, it seems that maybe I do have an obsession with trout. Especially wild trout. I don't think that my trouty obsession really qualifies as insanity, though. I prefer to think of it as more of a harmless madness. In fact, through the process of searching for Traver's magic, I've realized that I have somehow become attuned to his madness. Or maybe my new-found madness *is* the magic. Maybe that's why he titled his books in the order that he did. Because madness leads to magic, or the illusion of it. After all, magic and madness both are founded on mental illusions, or at least psychological quirks. In essence, chasing Traver's magic has somehow resulted in catching Traver's madness. In the end, I have found that magic and madness are often difficult to distinguish from each other anyway. Come to think of it, there really is no end to this magically maddening pursuit. At least not in this life.

I have found that my fascination, and apparent obsession, is just as much with the water and the unknowns that it shrouds as it is with the fish that live there. I've also realized that throughout my time chasing Traver's magic, I have developed a lot of connections—with people, streams, and geographic areas. I haven't quite figured out yet if those connections are part of the magic or if they are simply a result of the magic, or maybe even a means to the magic.

Trout magic is what many of us chase, though time and again we find that it's just beyond our reach. It is addictively fun to chase, but often frustratingly elusive. It may be lurking in far-away exotic locations, or the familiar stream next door. Moving water is typically where I find myself chasing the magic, but lakes and ponds are certainly not out of the question. Even big lakes, like Superior.

For me, sometimes the magic is in the moment, providing quick gratification. Other times it comes later, even much later, when I'm reliving the moment and noticing details I somehow didn't notice before. It's the same magic that I find in a peaceful wilderness evening, or a hushed glowing sunset on a remote lake with the cries of loons echoing across the water. It's in the prehistoric-sounding screams of a bull elk piercing the forest or echoing through a mountain valley. It's there when I'm looking into the wide eyes of an excited young child. It's that moment, or even a short string of moments, where everything seems right, and life feels good. It's that fleeting moment I yearn to hang onto and wish I could relive again and again. Who would think that a slimy cold-blooded creature could stir up such feelings?

The closest that I have come to actually catching the magic is when I feel the energetic dancing of a wild trout at the end of my line. And even then, it's a fleeting encounter. When I'm snagged on a log or my line is wrapped around a tree branch, I often wonder what happened to the magic of fly fishing for trout. The same thought roams my mind as mosquitoes are lining up on the knuckles of my casting hand, or when I am trying to thread my tippet through the eye of even a moderate-size fly on a day when I somehow forgot my flip-down magnifier at home. At the end of the primary fishing season, when my list of places that I wanted to fish still has numerous lines with no checkmark, or when I finally fish a bucket-list body of water and it doesn't even come close to my dreams, the magic feels far away, and I sometimes question if it's even real. Fortunately, those feelings tend to be short-lived, so I can soon ditch my little pity party and get my focus back on trouty pursuits with a fly rod.

Over time, I have come to find that the magic isn't something that can readily be caught. The magic, it seems, is in the chase. It's in slight movements in the bottom of a dark hole or current-blurred riffle. The planning of the next adventure, and the one after that. The pondering of benthic activities and apparitions. The enchanting voices of moving water. It is in the dreaming, the planning, the exploring. It is in the sight of an energetic steelhead pursuing your streamer into the shallows of a sandbar. The discovery of an eight-inch brookie calmly finning in a spot virtually impossible to fish. It is in the other streamside fauna and flora discovered during fishless times. Sometimes, it is even in plans laid to venture into new water, or wild adventurous ideas you're not sure are even feasible.

The magic is in carefully exploring a lake or stream with rod and reel. Plying its depths. Learning its features and unraveling some of its mysteries. The magic is in gaining a deeper understanding of the natural world we were created to be a part of, witnessing its miracles and participating in its flow. The magic is in getting to know our furred, feathered, and finned neighbors and the intricate environs they call home. Living in the moment while honing skills and regaining insights lost to modern civilization.

So, I have come to realize that the magic often has nothing to do with catching fish. Not that I have anything against catching fish. Especially trout. And it doesn't mean that I don't like catching fish. Catching fish, I have found, is an enjoyable thing to do, but it's merely a tangible fringe benefit. The magic is simply in the fishing. Or maybe it's more accurate to say that the magic is simply in the pursuit of fish, or the pursuit of something, and everything that pursuit entails. Catching and releasing some beautiful works of art or even enjoying a delicious meal now and then are only secondary gifts. Catching consists of pure fact. Chasing, on the other hand, is a misty blend of imagination and anticipation.

There have been days that I've caught numerous trout. Days that I have caught reasonably large trout or salmon. Days that I have fished bucket-list locations and streams that are trophies in and of themselves. In all those instances, the magic was there, but I somehow couldn't quite grasp it. I wasn't able to say that I achieved my goal or the success that I was chasing to where I could check it off the list. Call it complete. Through all my chasing after Traver's magic, I came to realize that the magic is in the chasing itself. It's an ephemeral thing that simply cannot be caught and held onto or kept as a possession. At first, that was a source of much frustration, but I have more recently come to realize it as a blessing, because no matter what I accomplish from a trout fishing or fly fishing standpoint, the chase will never be over. It will always be in front of me. There will always be a need for the chase. A yearning for the pursuit and all that it entails. The chase doesn't end until the mind and body are no longer capable of chasing. Until then, those of us caught up in the allure of fly fishing for trout can continue to revel in the madness of chasing the magic.

ABOUT THE AUTHOR

For more than five decades John Highlen has been enjoying pursuits such as hiking, hunting, fishing, backpacking, canoeing, kayaking, exploring, and climbing, as well as many others. Though John's fly rod days have only spanned the last dozen or so years, his passion for trout and the waters they call home began burning back in the days of his youth. The many years spent absorbed in the outdoors, experiencing nature from numerous perspectives, has given him a deep appreciation of and respect for our natural world. As a degreed mechanical engineer, John is able to recognize and understand the details of what he sees and how those details work together in the grand scheme. Overall, this eclectic blend of skills and experience allows him to see and interpret the natural world through a unique set of eyes. John strives to use those skills and experience in his writing to help connect readers with the natural world everyone is meant to be a part of and all the intrinsic benefits that flow from that connection. In 2016, John was blessed to be able to turn his attention full-time to outdoor adventures, writing, volunteering for conservation organizations and being the support crew for his wife, Julie's, art studio.

In 2019, John had the privilege of being an artist-in-residence with the *Listening Point Foundation*, in Ely Minnesota. There, he focused his writings on Sigurd Olson's beloved Listening Point and the nearby Boundary Waters Canoe Area Wilderness.

In 2020, He and Julie were each blessed with an artist-in-residence with the *Friends of the Porkies*. Having an opportunity to live a simple life in the Porcupine Mountains wilderness for more than a month that year, focusing on interpreting his outdoors experiences, helped solidify John's desire to write.

In addition to a number of outdoors-related articles, John has published two other non-fiction outdoor adventure books, *Touching the Wild U.P.* and *Porkies Wilderness Wanderings*. Both books are available through Amazon, as well as most local bookstores.

John and his wife enjoy living in Deerton, Michigan, in a home surrounded by woods, less than ten minutes from the wonders of Lake Superior. From this vantage point, they paint the wilds of the north woods and waters to share nature's inspiration with others— Julie with brush and canvas, John with pen and paper.

9 798990 030701